VOLUPTUOUS VICES

50 SEXPLOITATION & ADULT FILM POSTERS FROM ITALY

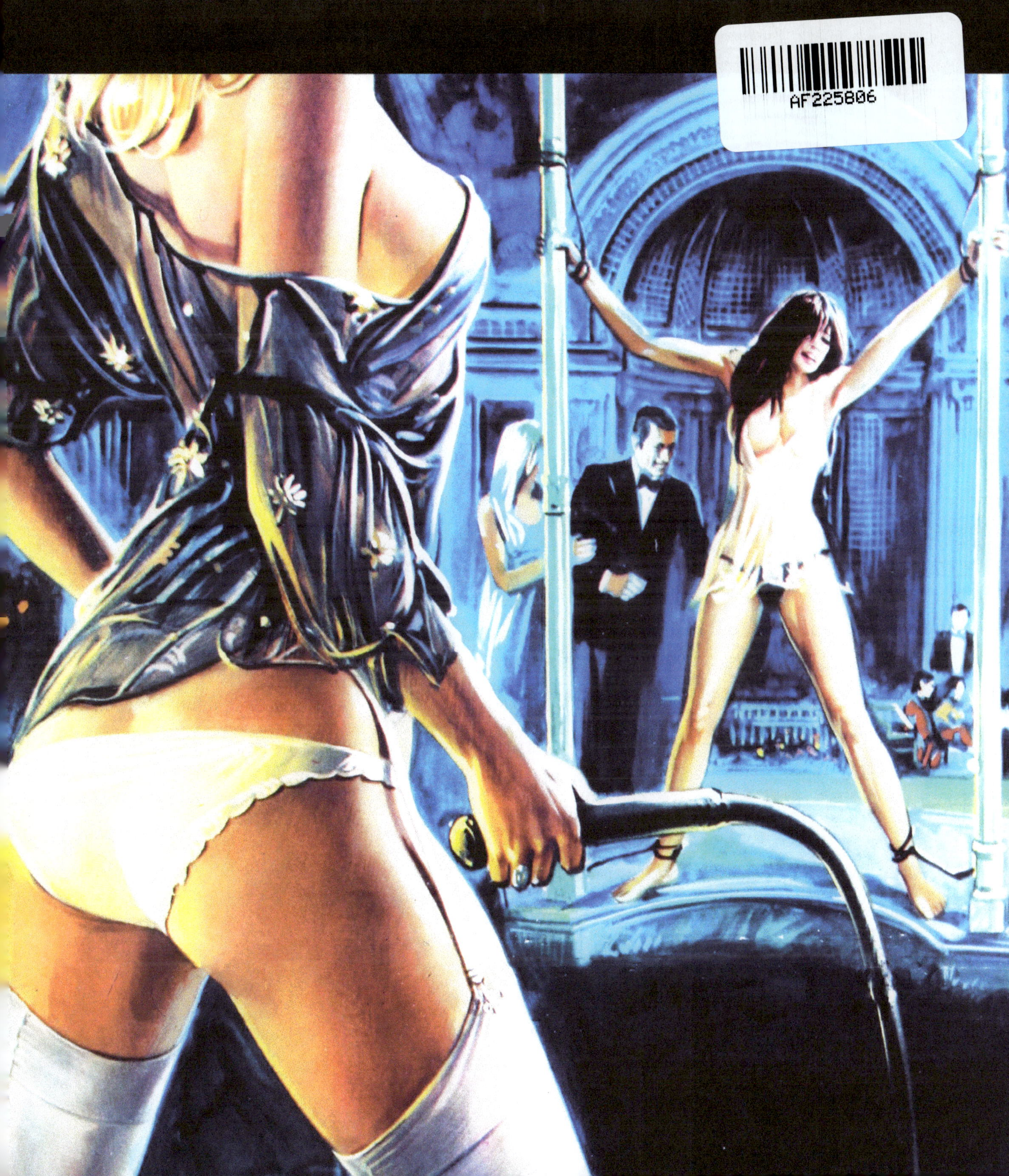

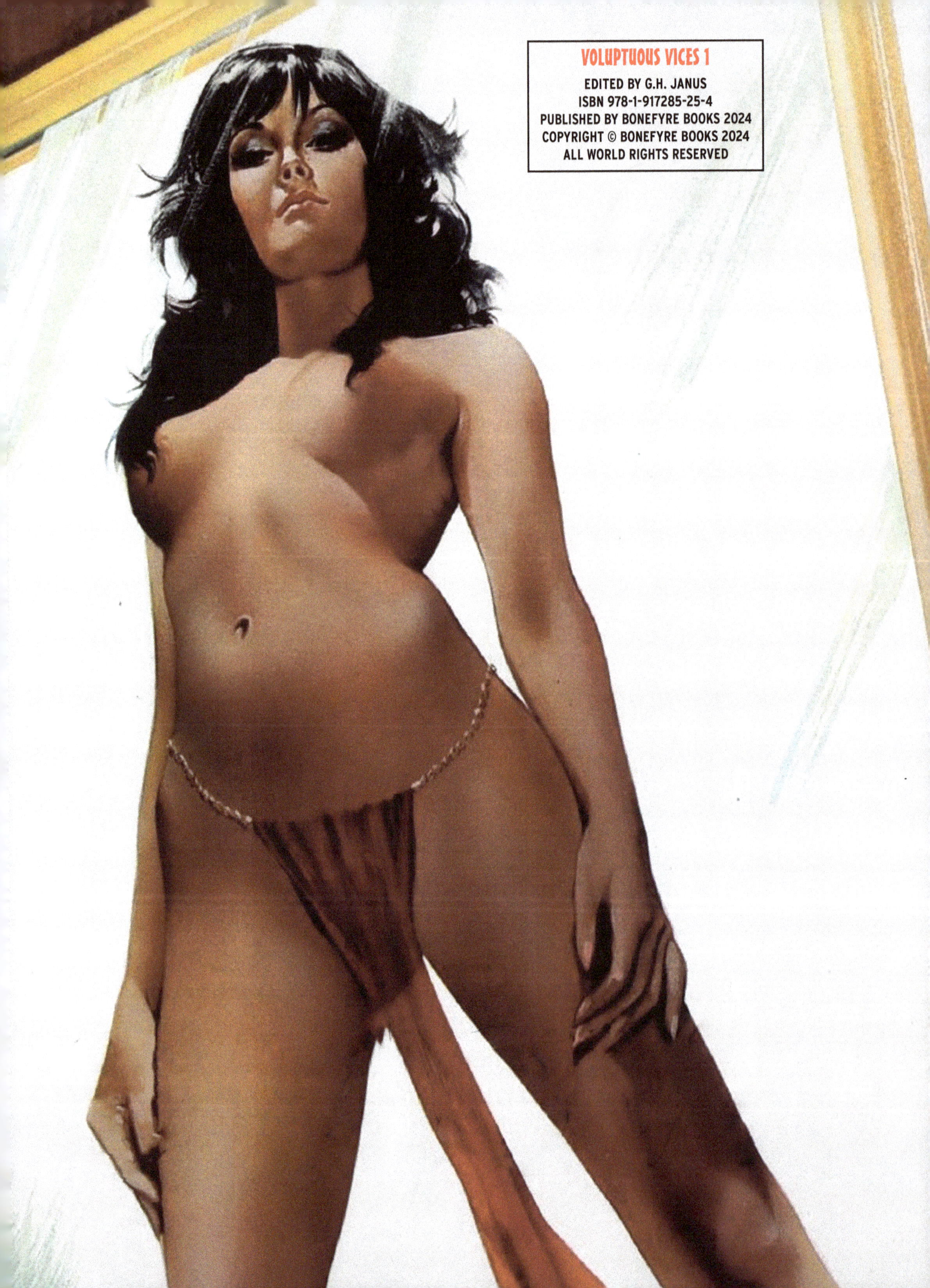
VOLUPTUOUS VICES 1
EDITED BY G.H. JANUS
ISBN 978-1-917285-25-4
PUBLISHED BY BONEFYRE BOOKS 2024
COPYRIGHT © BONEFYRE BOOKS 2024
ALL WORLD RIGHTS RESERVED

POSTERS

LE MAGNIFICHE FALENE DI GINZA — 4
GLI ADORATORI DEL SESSO — 5
IO, EMMANUELLE — 6
BRUCIA RAGAZZO BRUCIA — 7
DIO ME L'HA DATA, GUAI A CHI LA TOCCA — 8
GIOCHI EROTICI IN DANIMARCA — 9
GUARDAMI NUDA — 10
I 7 DESIDERI DI UNA VERGINE — 11
NEL PARADISO DEL PIACERE — 12
L'HO SORPRESO A LETTO CON UN'ALTRA — 13
PORNO ESPERIENZE EROTICHE — 14
CLUB PRIVE... PER COPPIE RAFFINATE! — 15
PIACERI EROTICI DI UNA SIGNORA-BENE — 16
SESSO RIBELLE — 17
TI PREGO... AMORE MIO SCALDAMI — 18
LA PORNO NINFOMANE — 19
LA NINFOMANE PORNO — 20
EROS SUPERSEX — 21
PECCATI SUL LETTO DI FAMIGLIA — 22
CLITO ORGASMO BAGNATO — 23
PORNO HOLIDAYS — 24
STORIA DI EMMANUELLE "O": IL TRIONFO DELL'EROTISMO — 25
LA SEGRETARIA — 26
LA PORNOCAROVANA — 27
EMANUELLE NERA — 28
FATELO CON ME... BIONDE DOLCI DANESI — 29
SHOCKING — 30
OSINDA VIZIO E PECCATO — 31
PIACERI FOLLI — 32
SEX EMOTION — 33
SONO EROTICA, SONO SEXY, SONO PORNO! — 34
PORNO SHOCK — 35
JULIE BLUE PORNO STORY — 36
PORNODELIRIO — 37
LE RAGAZZE BLUE PORNO — 38
EMANUELLE E LOLITA — 39
PIACERI PROIBITI DI UNA DONNA DI CLASSE — 40
SEX EXIBITION — 41
CIVILTA DEL VIZIO — 42
INSAZIABILI NOTTI DI UNA NINFOMANE — 43
QUELLO STRANO DESIDERIO — 44
PORCO MONDO (PORNO) — 45
TORBIDI DESIDERI DI UNA NINFOMANE — 46
PERVERSIONE EROTICA DI UNA MINORENNE — 47
LE PICCOLE COLLEGIALE — 48
VITA SCABROSA DI UNA PROSTITUTA — 49
PORNO HOLOCAUST — 50
FURIA EROTICA — 51
FOLLI PIACERI DELLE PORNO PRIGIONIERE — 52
MARINA PERVERSA — 53

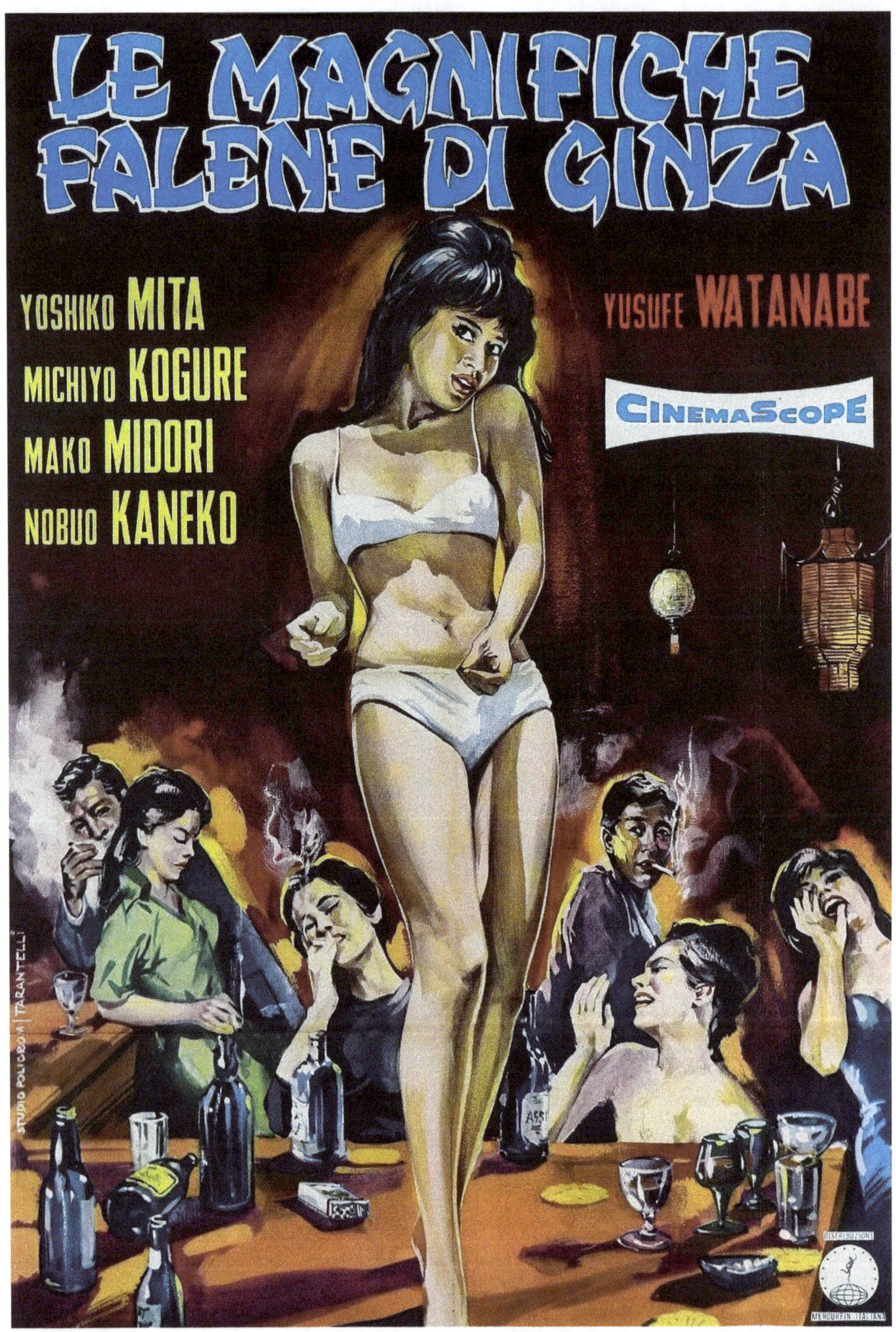

LE MAGNIFICHE
FALENE DI GINZA
YOSHIKO MITA
MICHIYO KOGURE
MAKO MIDORI
NOBUO KANEKO
YUSUFE WATANABE
CinemaScope

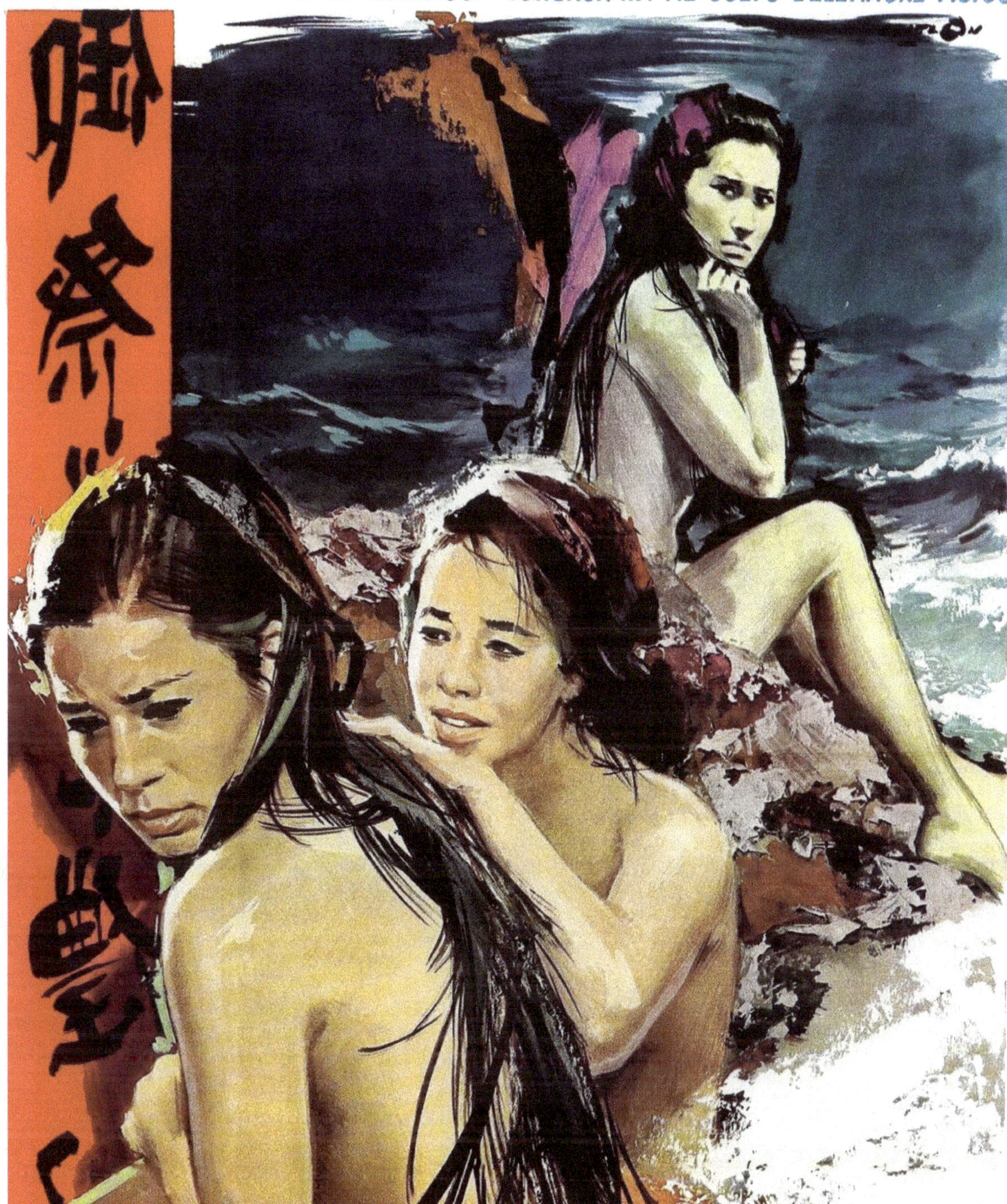

GLI ADORATORI DEL SESSO

Artist: Angelo Cessalon. Original Title: **Ensetsu Meiji Jakyo-Den** (1968).

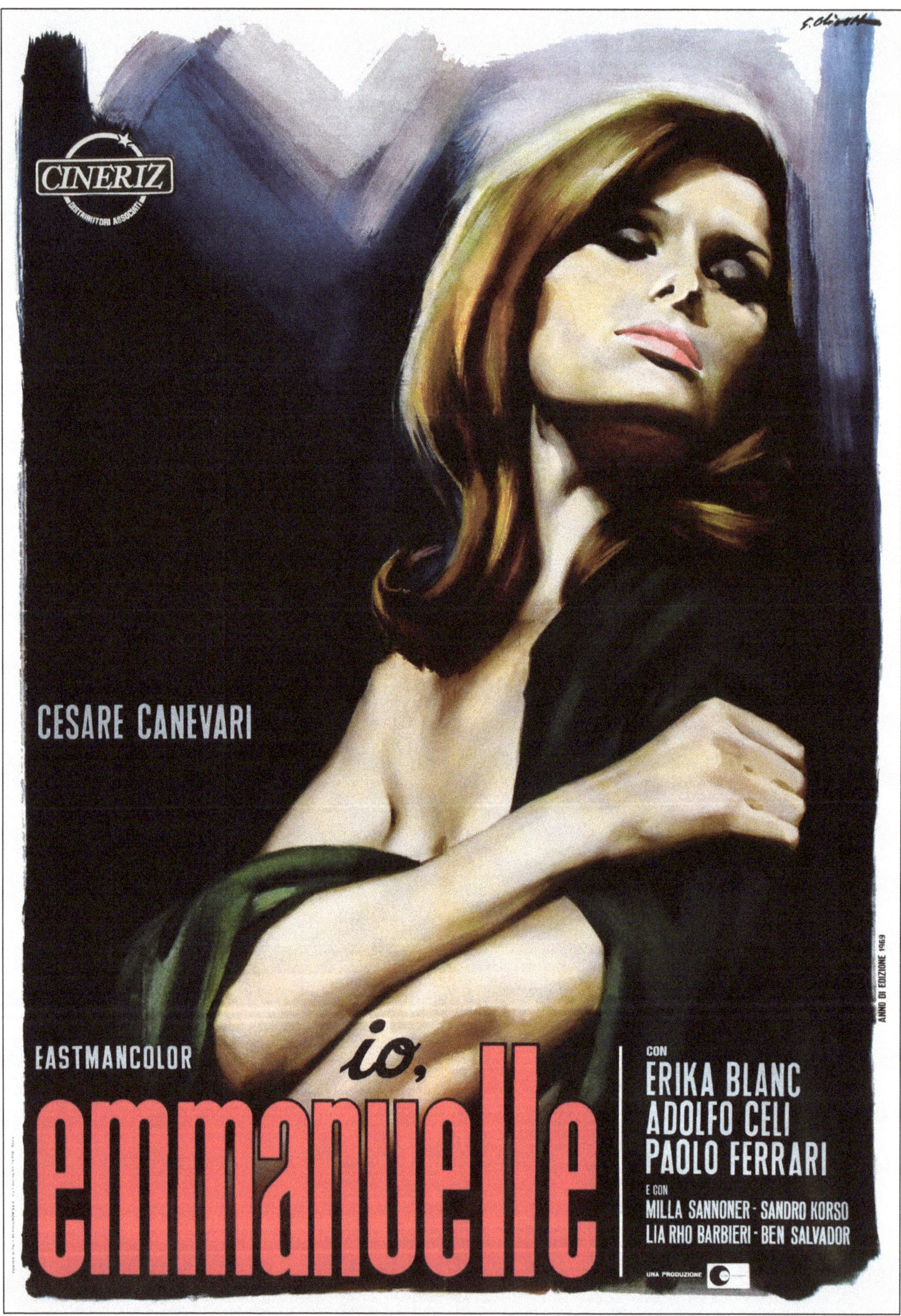

IO, EMMANUELLE

Artist: Giorgio Olivetti. Original Title: **Io, Emmanuelle** (1969).

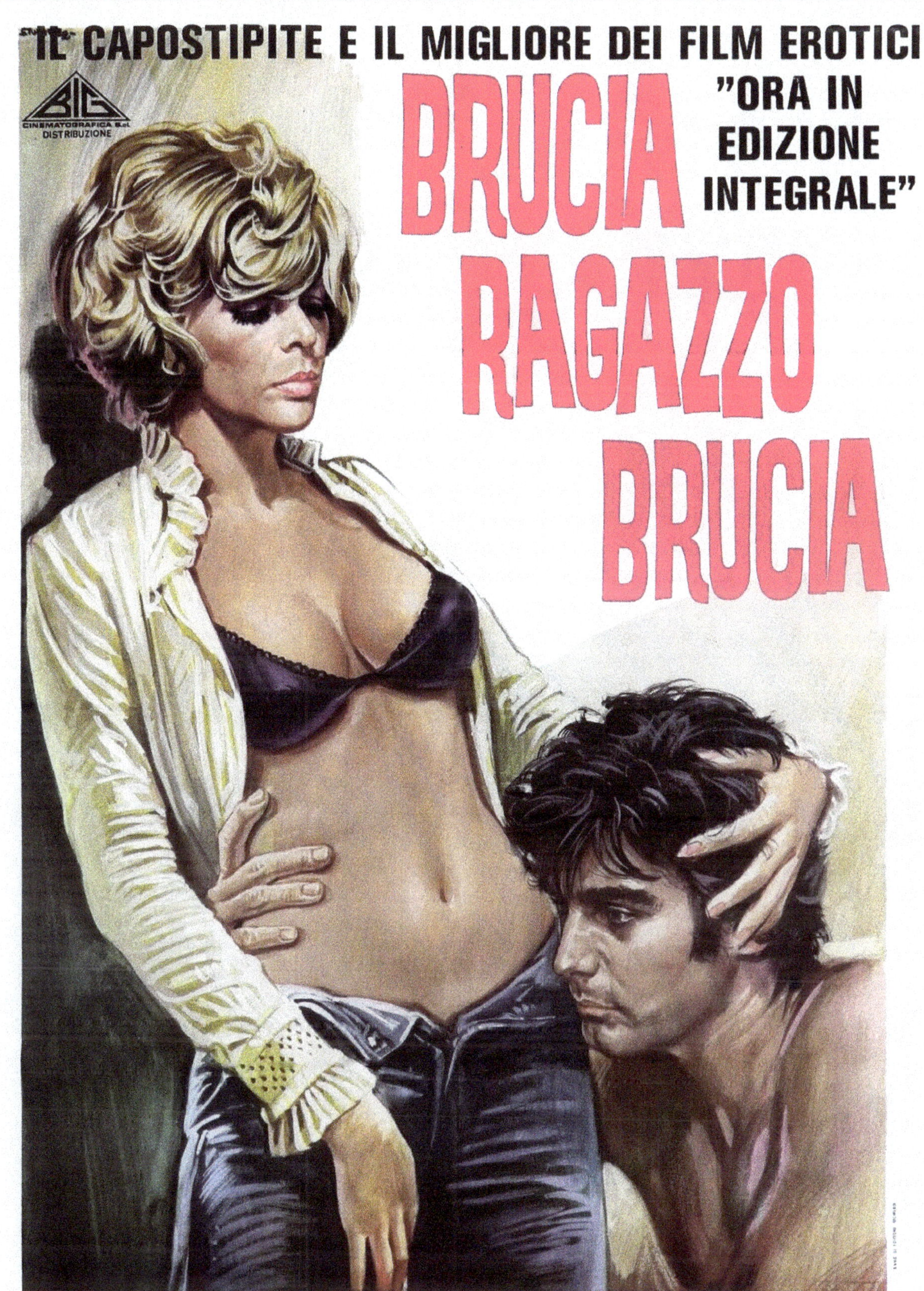

BRUCIA RAGAZZO BRUCIA

Artist: unsigned. Original Title: **Brucia Ragazzo Brucia** (1969).

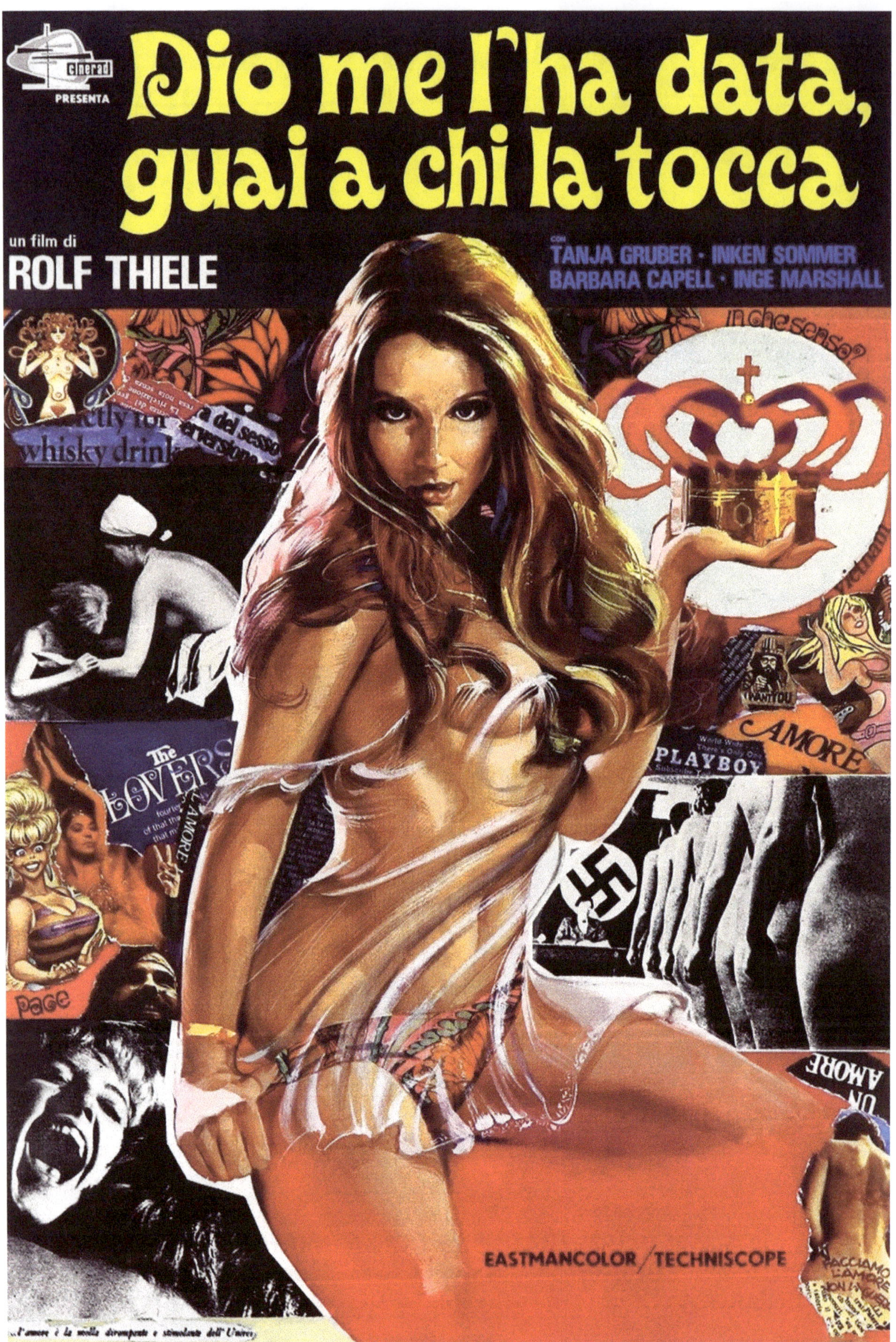

DIO ME L'HA DATA, GUAI A CHI LA TOCCA
Artist: unsigned. Original Title: **Komm Nur, Mein Liebstes Vogelein (1968).**

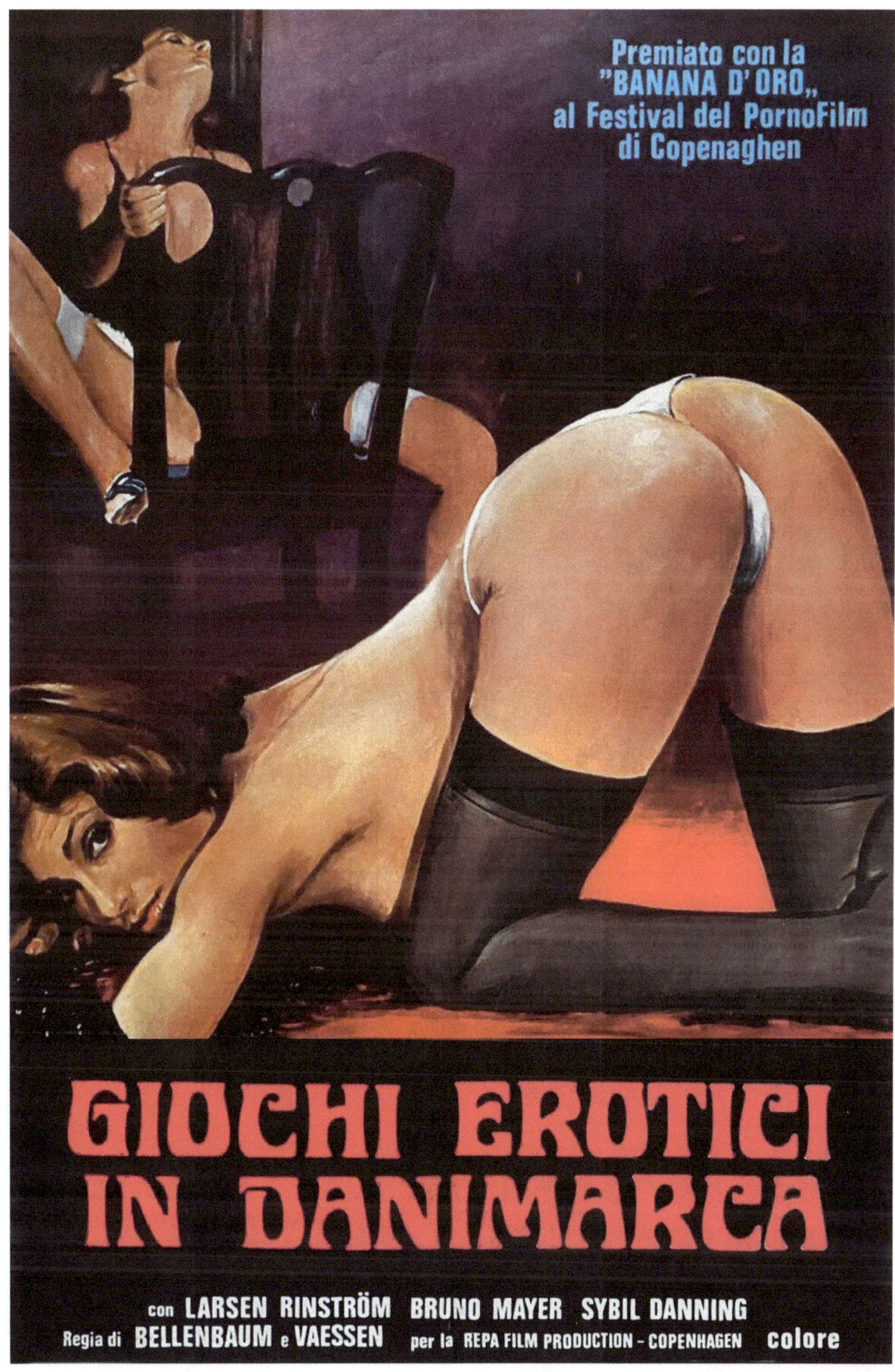

GIOCHI EROTICI IN DANIMARCA
Artist: unsigned. Original Title: **Liebesmarkt In Danemark (1971)**.

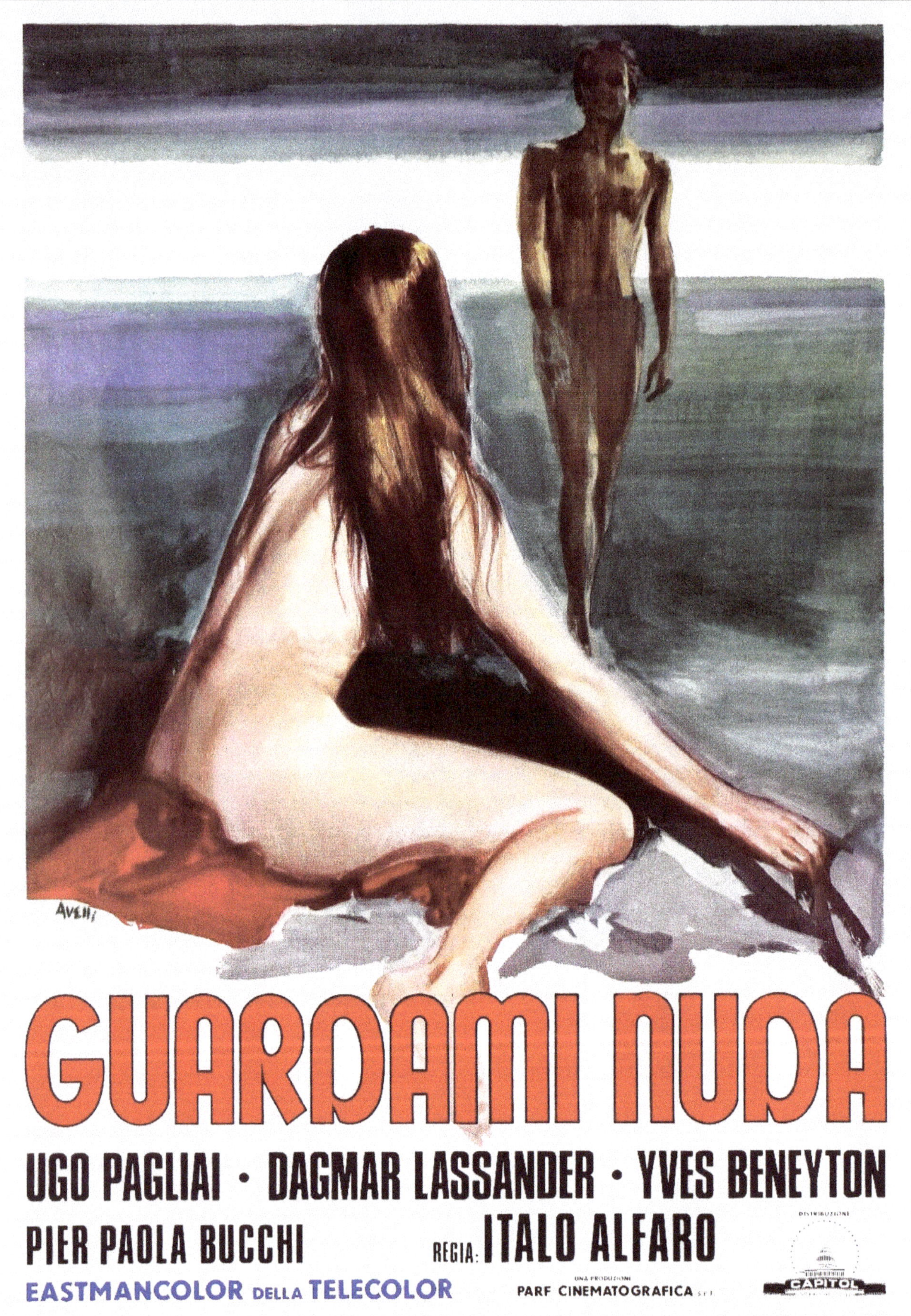

Artist: Tino Avelli. Original Title: **Guardami Nuda** (1972).

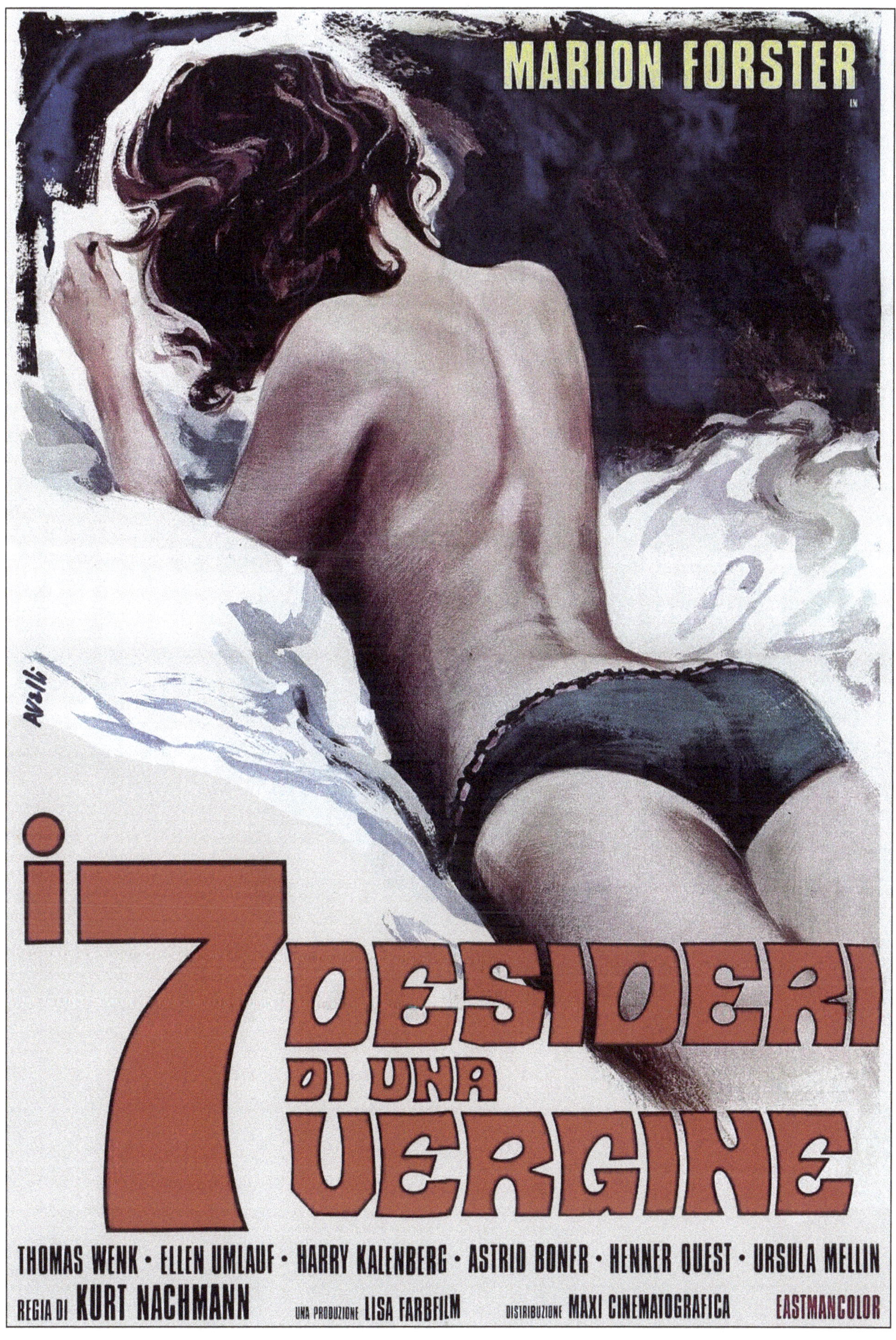

Artist: Tino Avelli. Original Title: **Auch Fummeln Will Gelernt Sein** (1972).

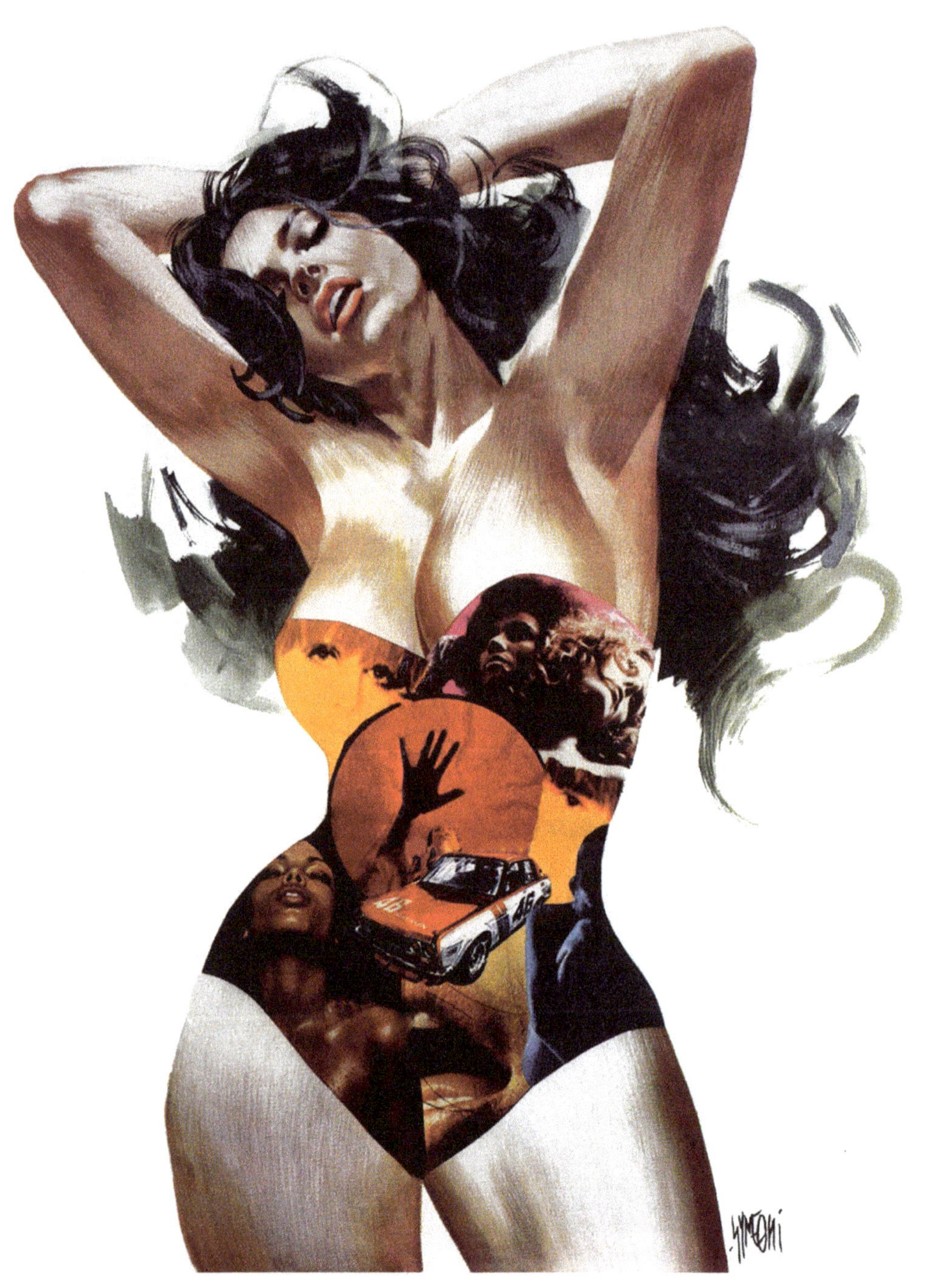

NEL PARADISO DEL PIACERE

Artist: Sandro Symeoni. Original Title: **La Maffia Du Plaisir** (1971).

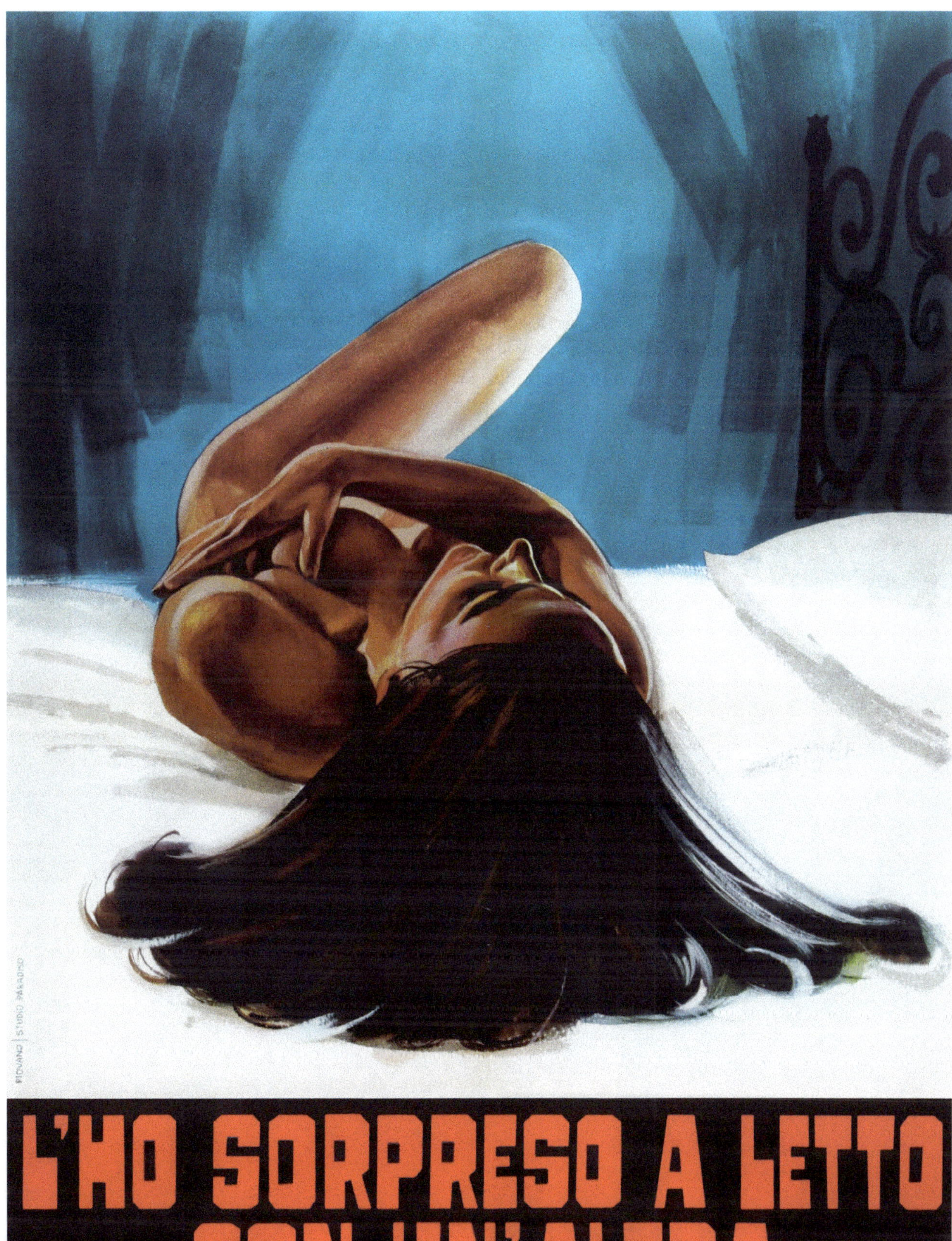

Artist: Mario Piovano (Studio Paradiso). Original Title: **Perverse Et Docile** (1971).

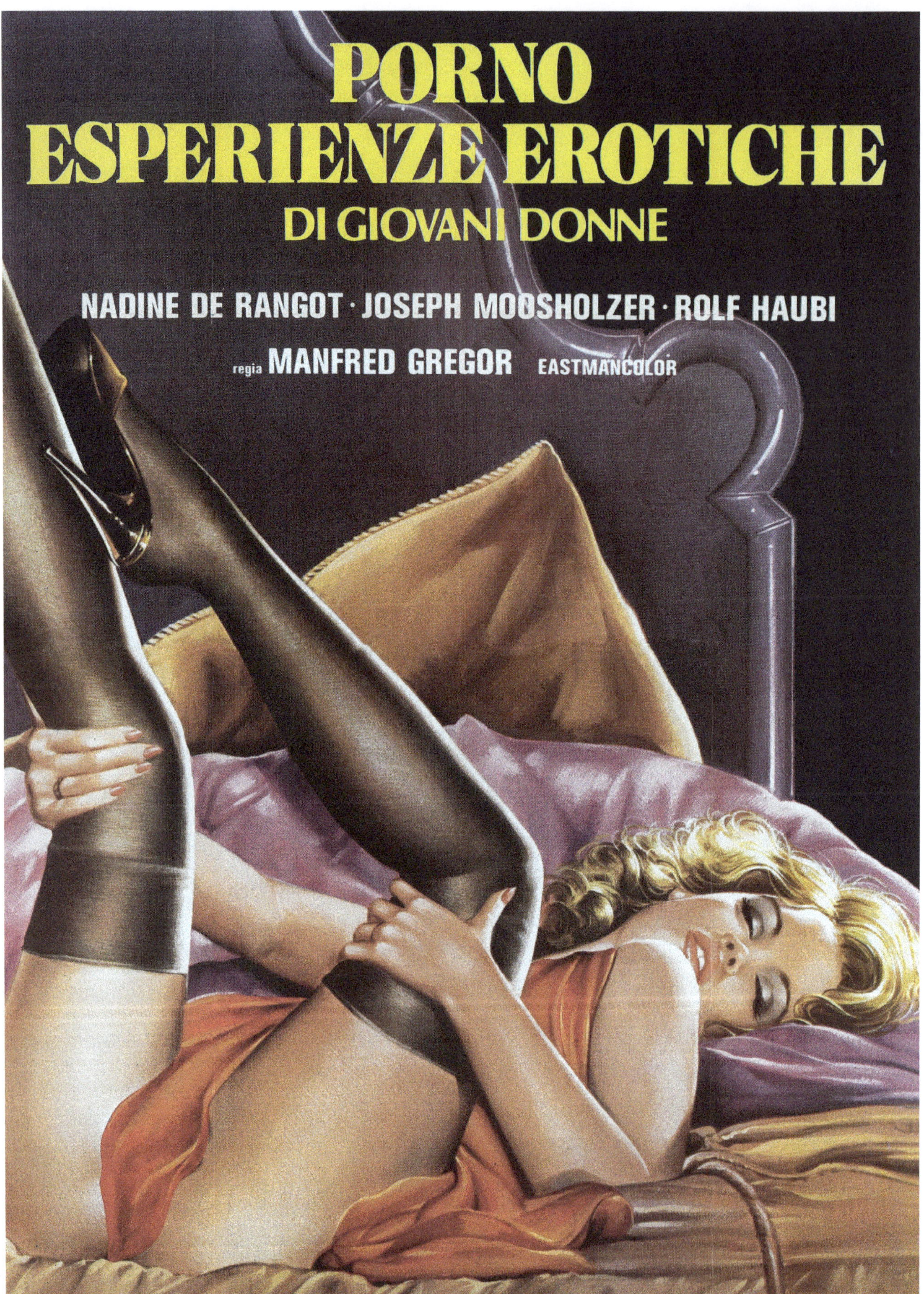

PORNO ESPERIENZE EROTICHE

Artist: unsigned. Original Title: **Die Madchenhandler** (1972).

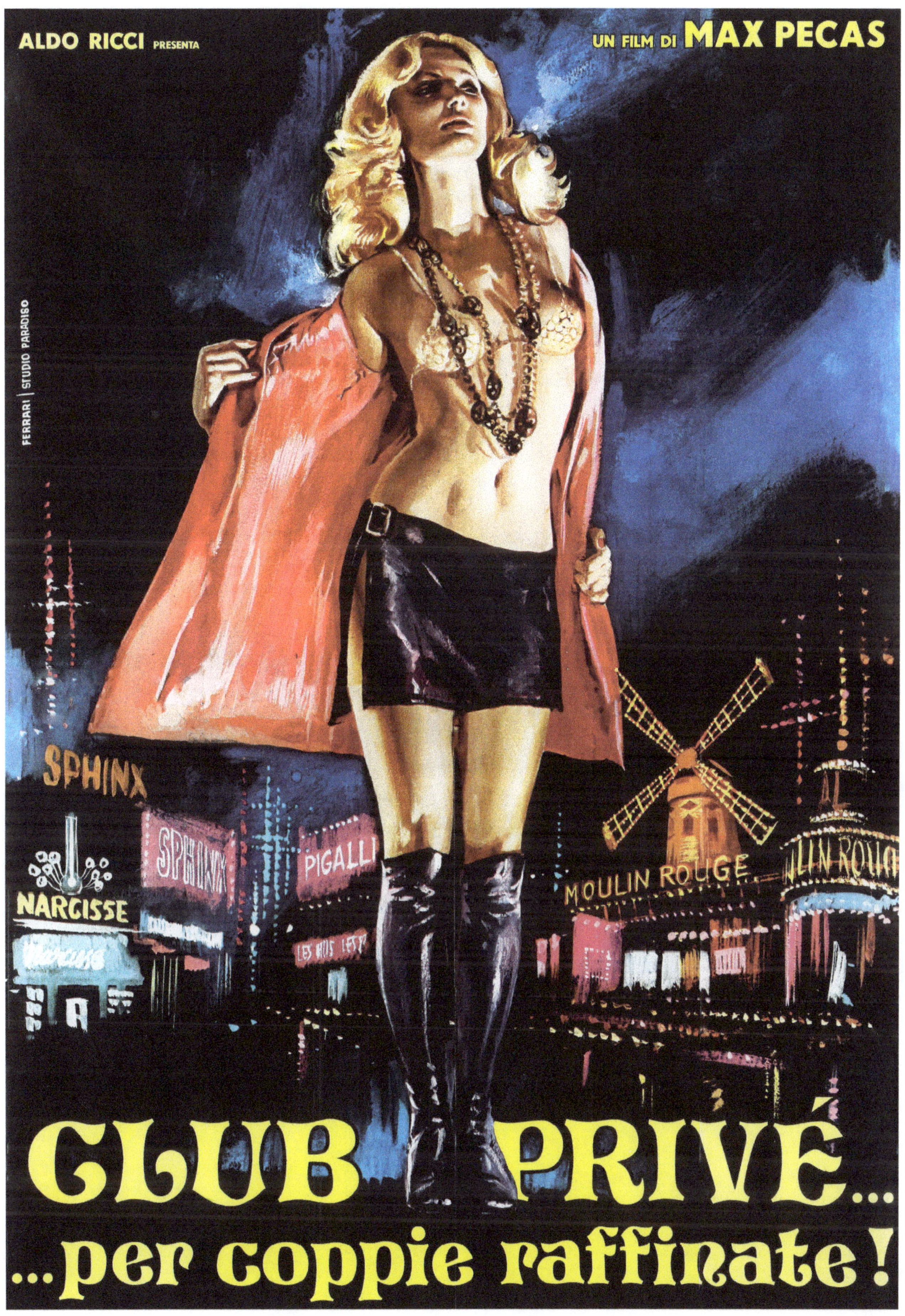

ALDO RICCI PRESENTA
UN FILM DI MAX PECAS
FERRARI | STUDIO PARADISO
SPHINX
NARCISSE
SPHINX
PIGALLI
LES BUS LESS
MOULIN ROUGE
MOULIN ROUGE
CLUB PRIVÉ...
...per coppie raffinate!

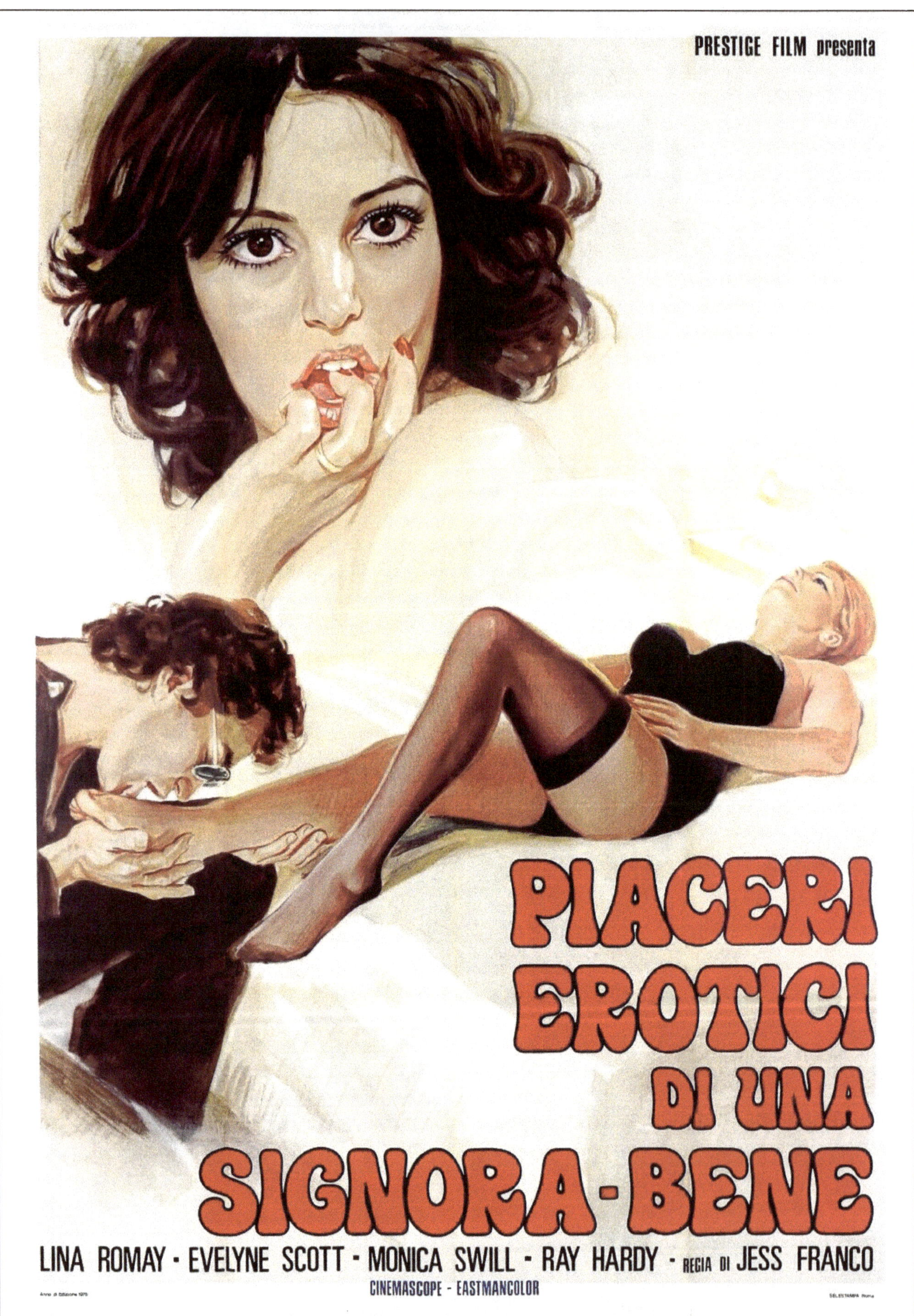

PIACERI EROTICI DI UNA SIGNORA-BENE

Artist: unsigned. Original Title: **Die Blonde Mit Dem Snessen Busen** (1974).

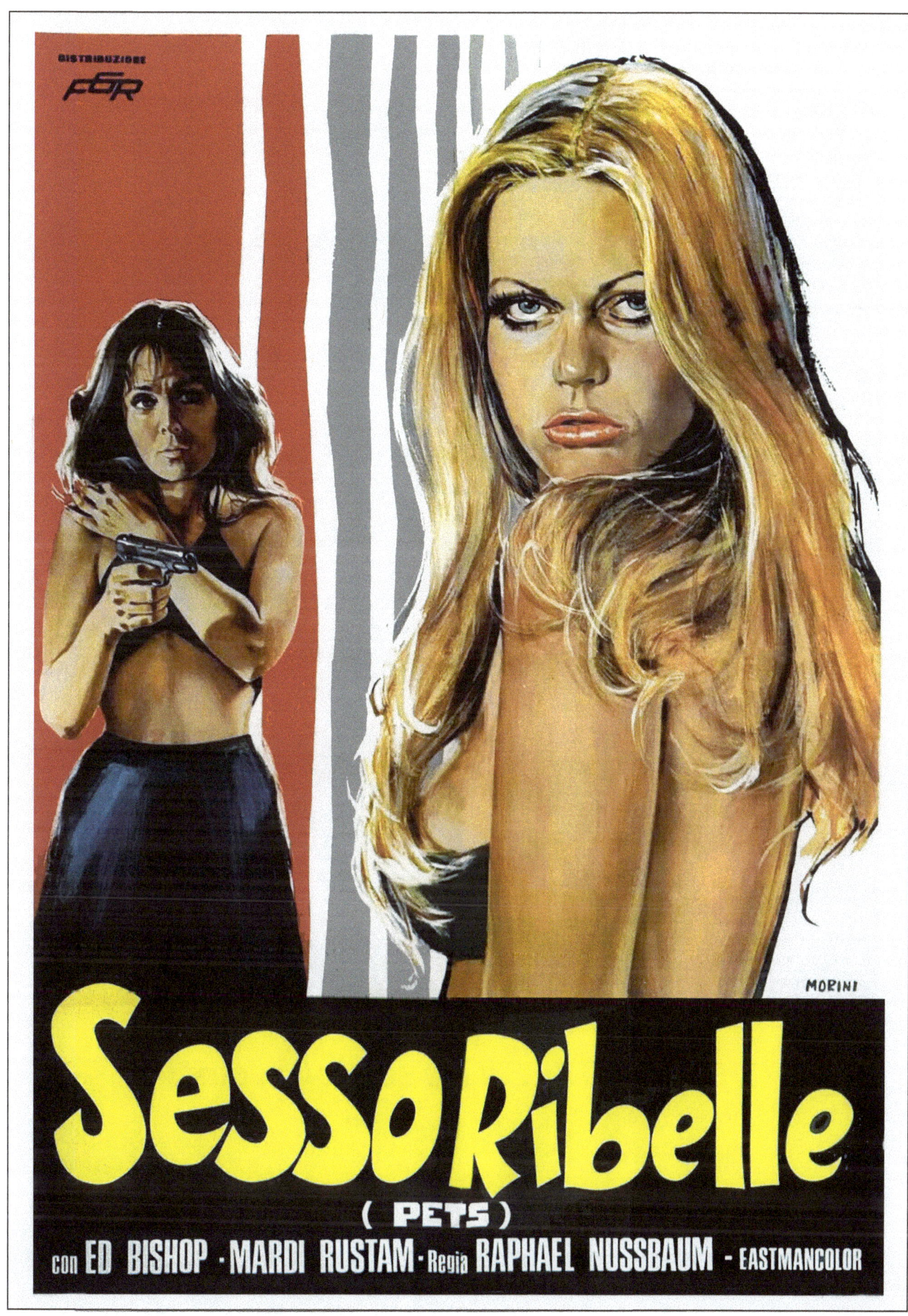

DISTRIBUZIONE
FGR
SessoRibelle
(PETS)
con ED BISHOP · MARDI RUSTAM · Regia RAPHAEL NUSSBAUM · EASTMANCOLOR
MORINI

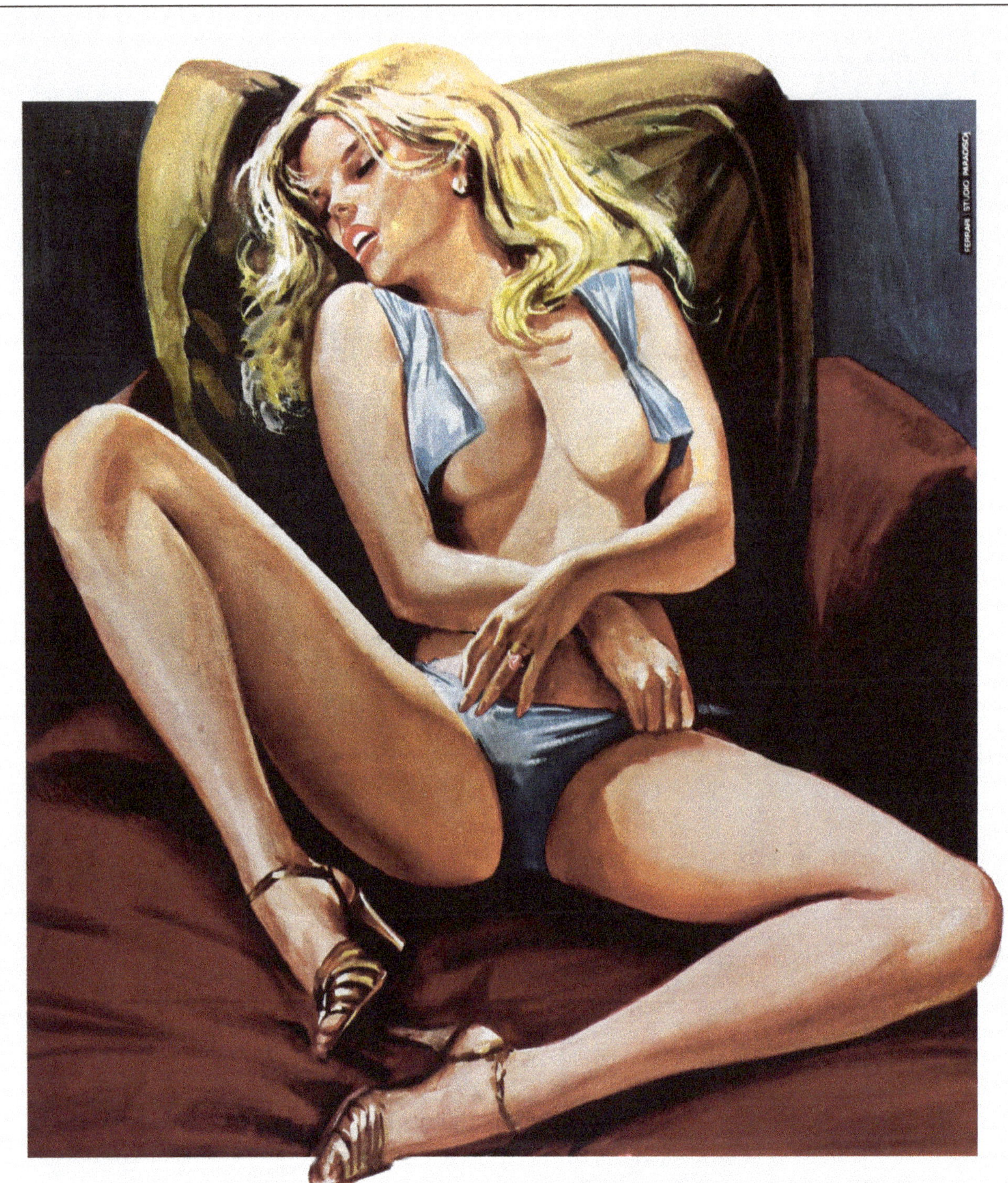

TI PREGO... AMORE MIO SCALDAMI

Artist: Ferrari (Studio Paradiso). Original Title: **Je Suis Frigide... Pourquoi?** (1972).

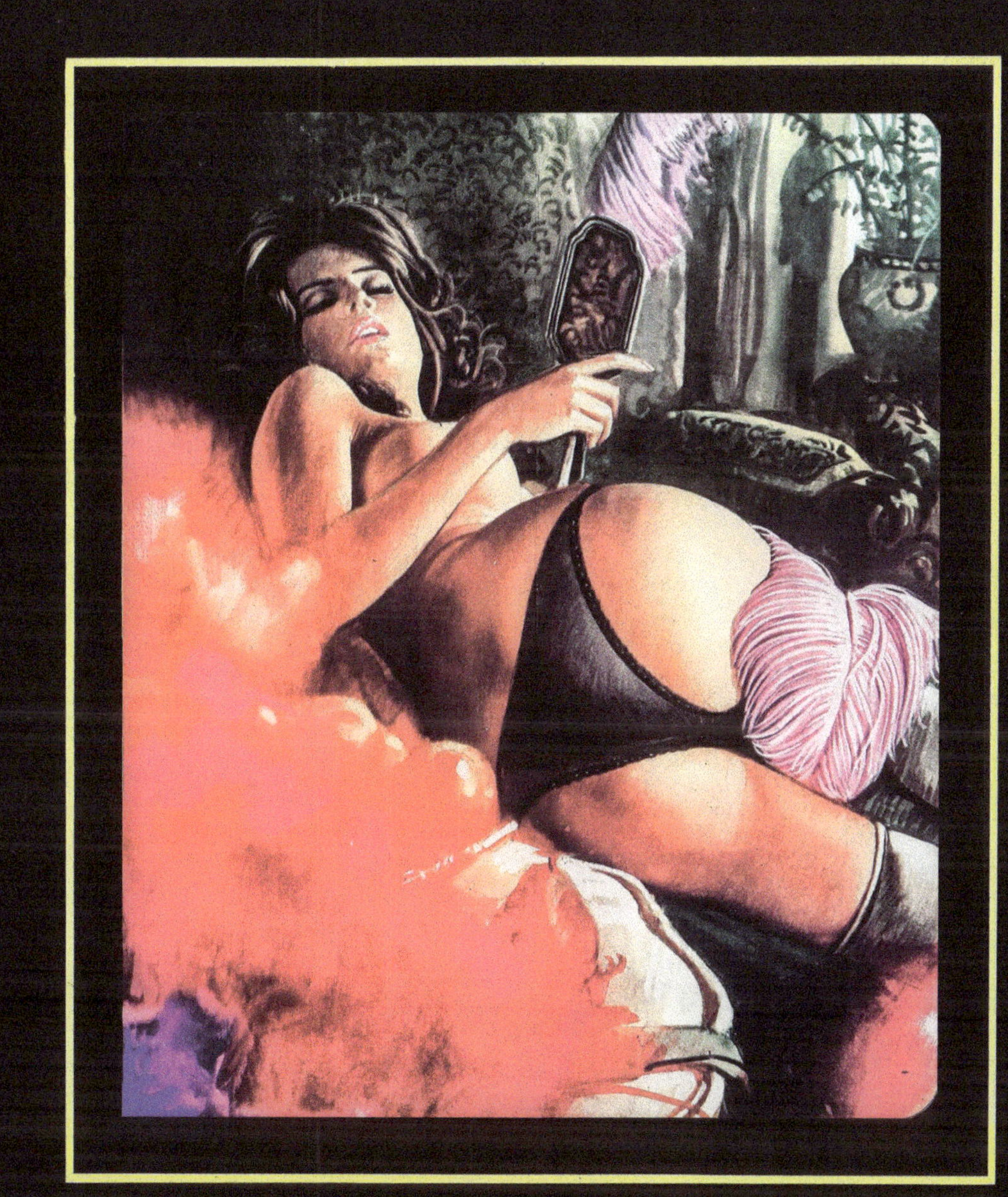

LA PORNO NINFOMANE
con MONIQUE VITA • J.M. DHERMAY • ANNE LIBERT
OLIVIER MATHOT • SYLVIE SOLAR • ROBERT AUDRAN
ALAIN BOUVETTE • regia: JEAN LEVITTE
una produzione P.C.P. - Parigi • EASTMANCOLOR

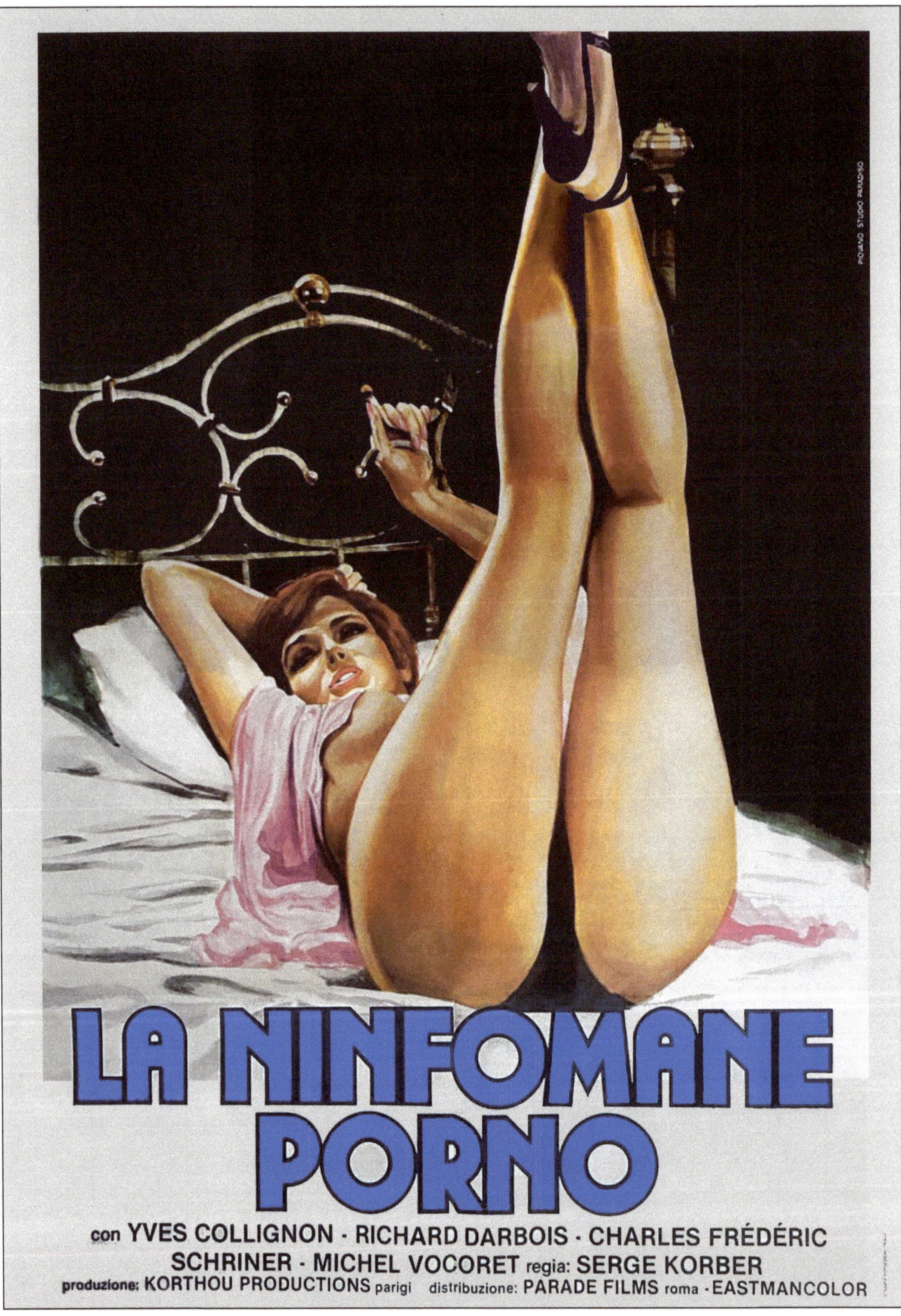

LA NINFOMANE PORNO

Artist: Mario Piovano (Studio Paradiso). Original Title: **A Bout De Sexe** (1975).

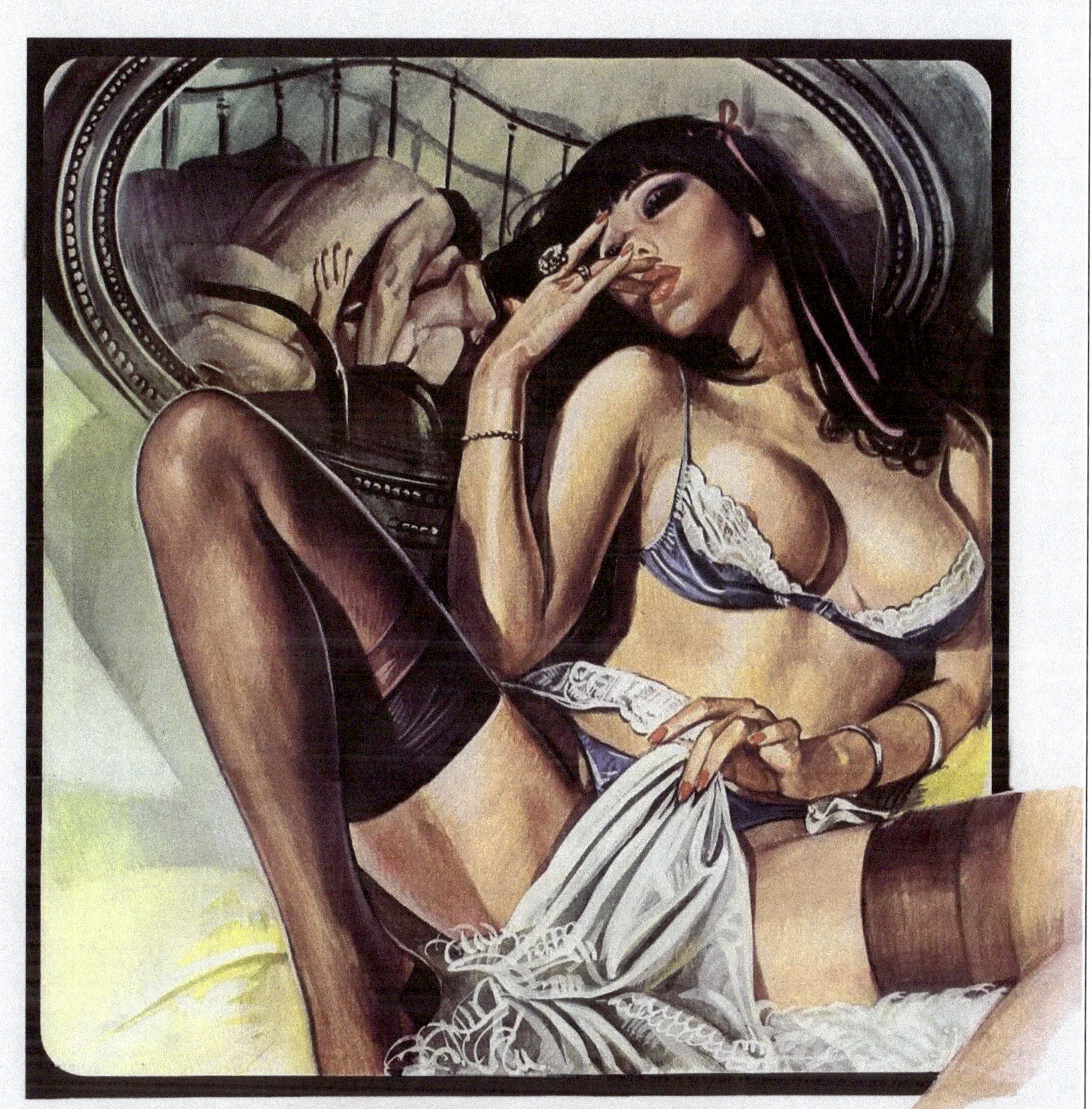

Artist: unsigned. Original Title: **Tour De Sexe** (1974).

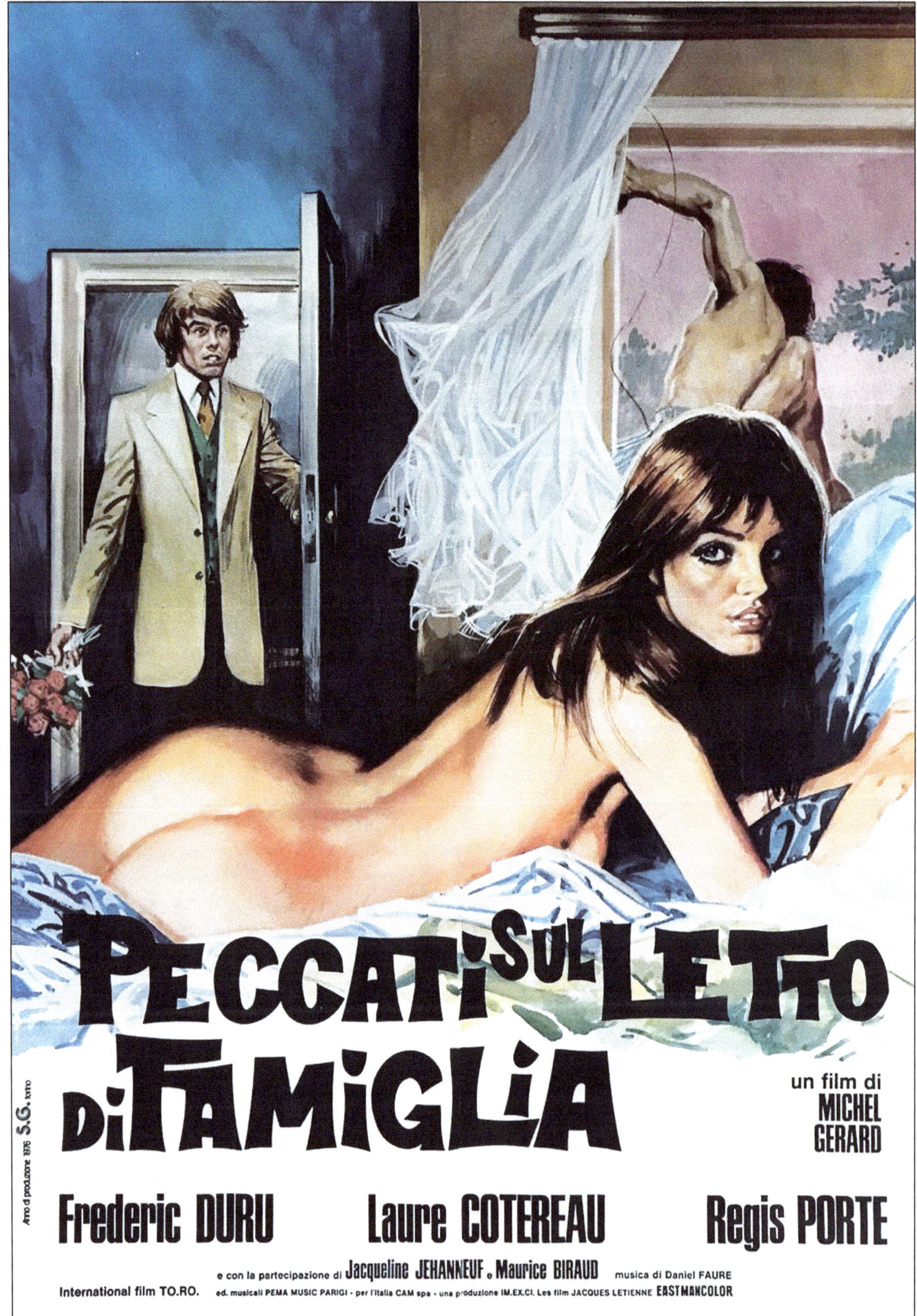

PECCATI SUL LETTO DI FAMIGLIA

Artist: unsigned. Original Title: **Salut Les Frangines** (1976).

CLITÒ ORGASMO BAGNATO

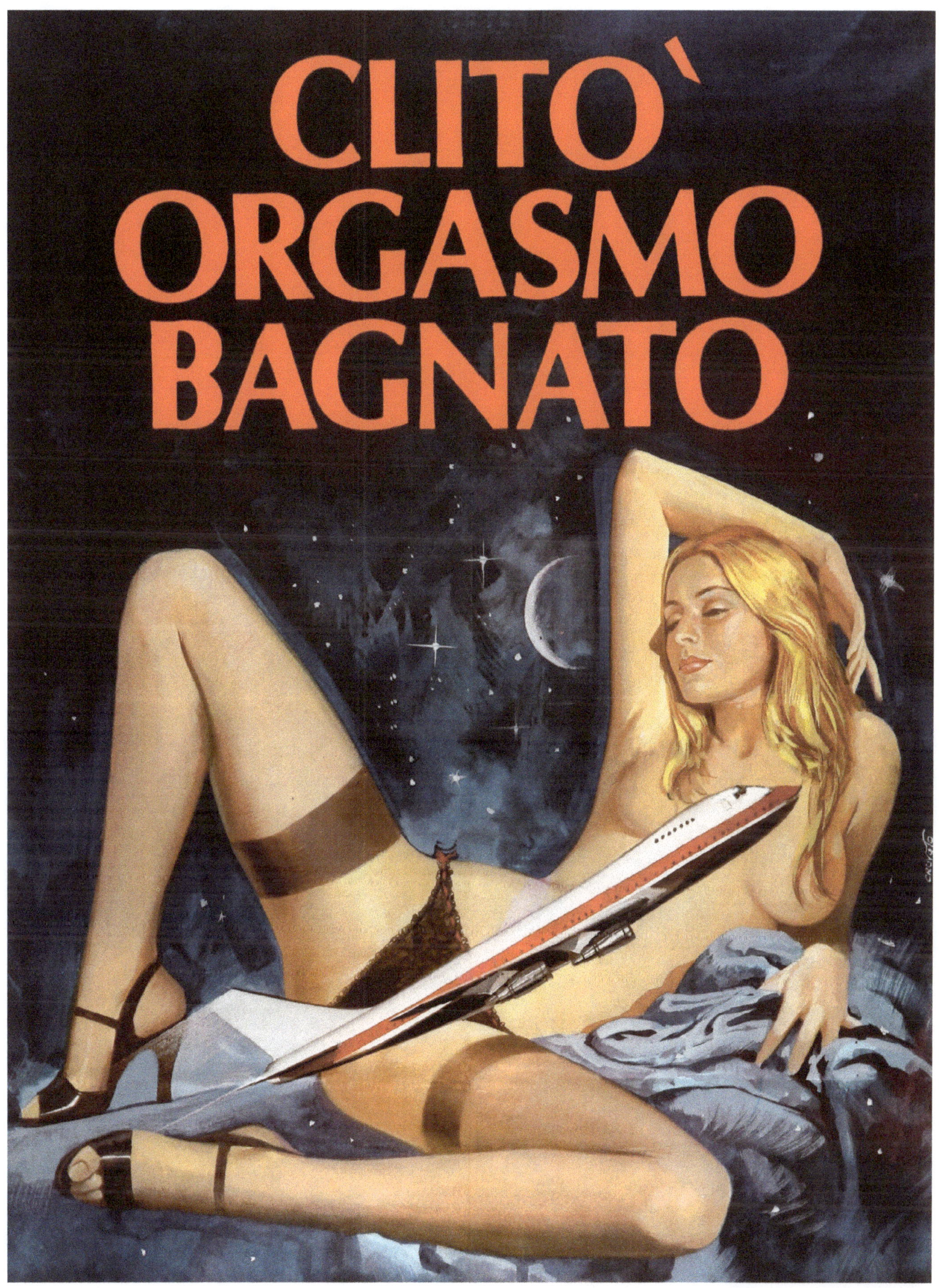

CLITO ORGASMO BAGNATO

Artist: Luca Crovato. Original Title: **J'Ai Tres Envie** (1975).

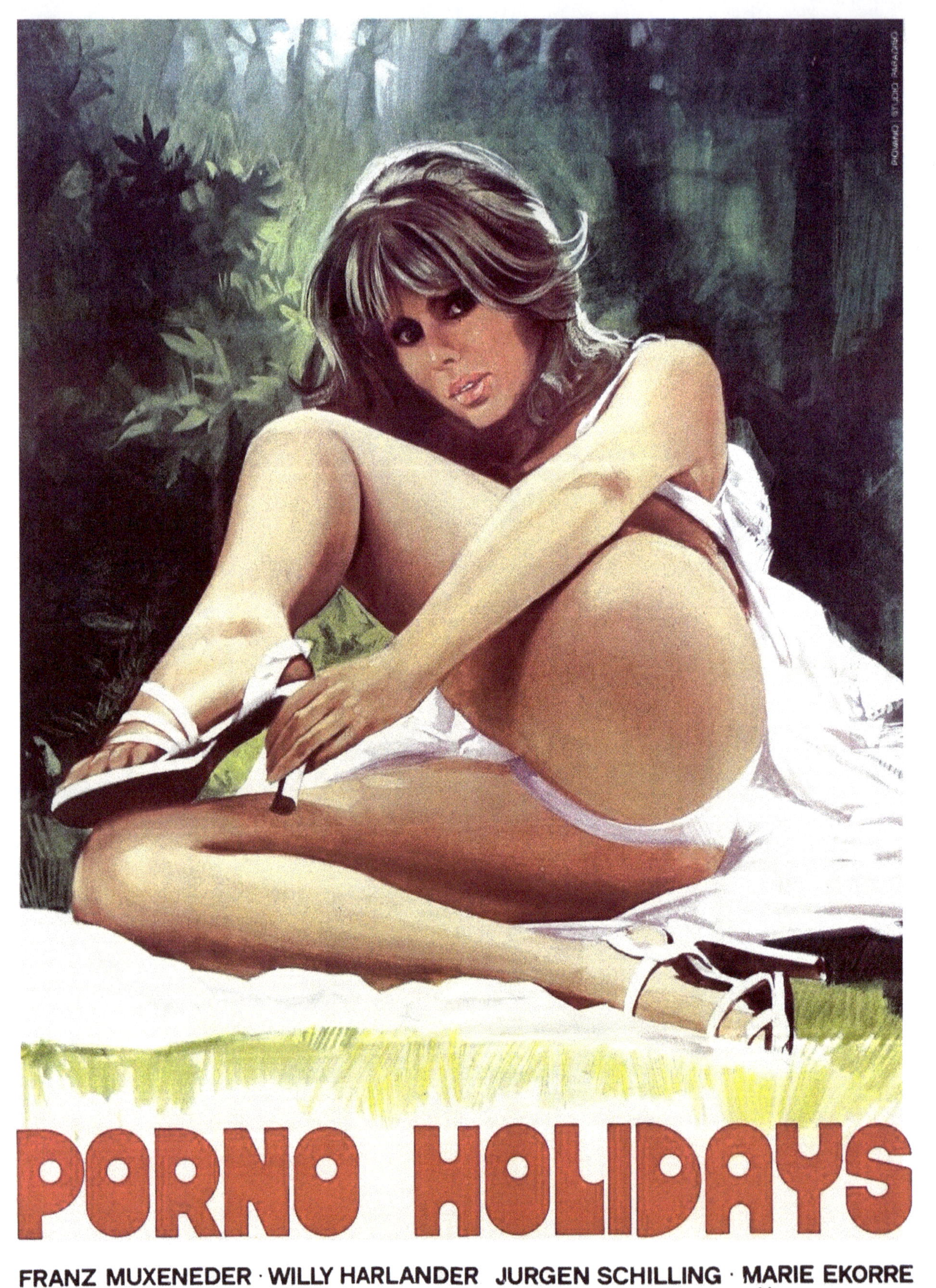

PORNO HOLIDAYS

Artist: Mario Piovano (Studio Paradiso). Original Title: **Was Treibt Die Maus Im Badehaus?** (1976).

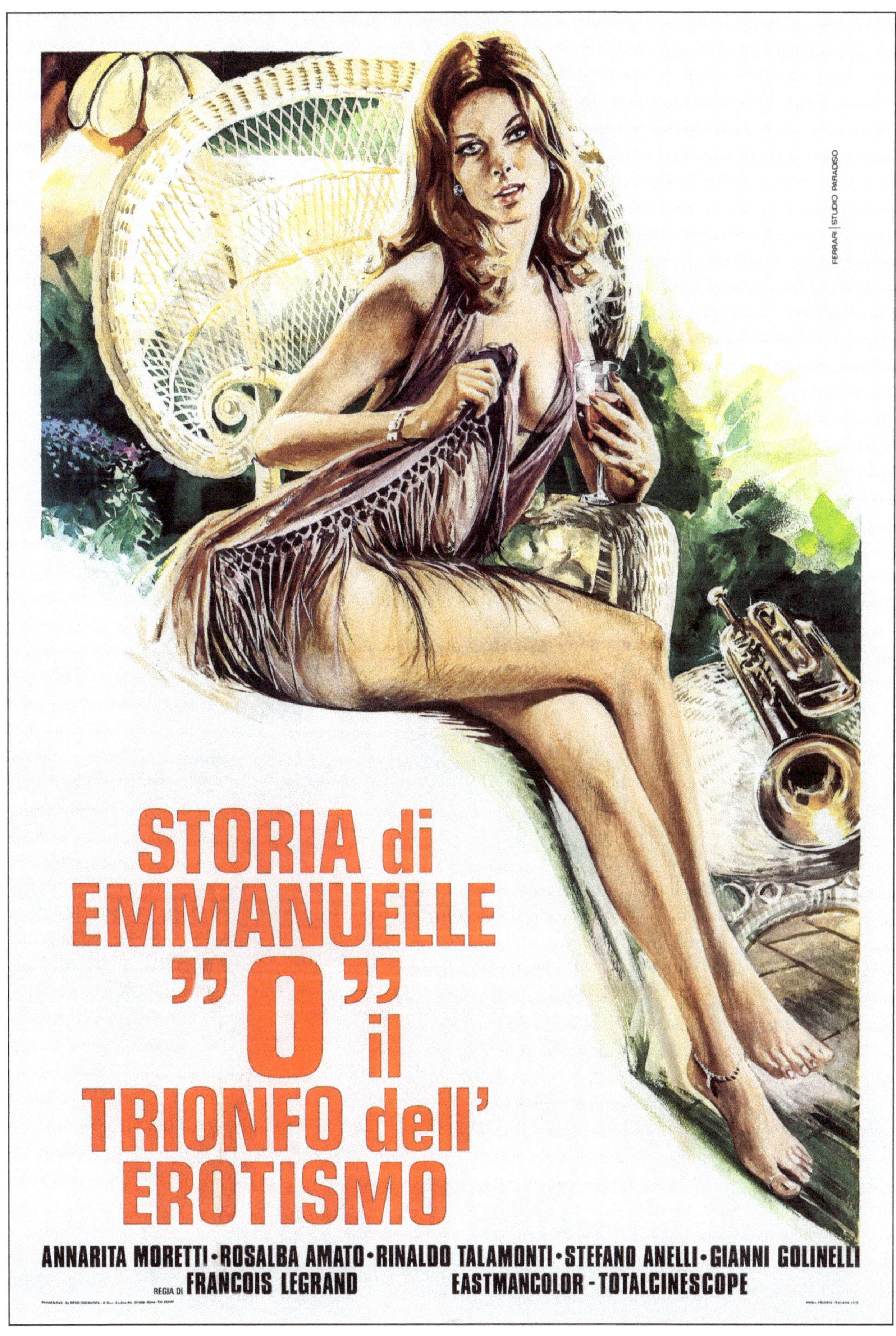

FERRARI | STUDIO PARADISO
STORIA di EMMANUELLE "O" il TRIONFO dell' EROTISMO
ANNARITA MORETTI · ROSALBA AMATO · RINALDO TALAMONTI · STEFANO ANELLI · GIANNI GOLINELLI
REGIA DI FRANCOIS LEGRAND
EASTMANCOLOR - TOTALCINESCOPE

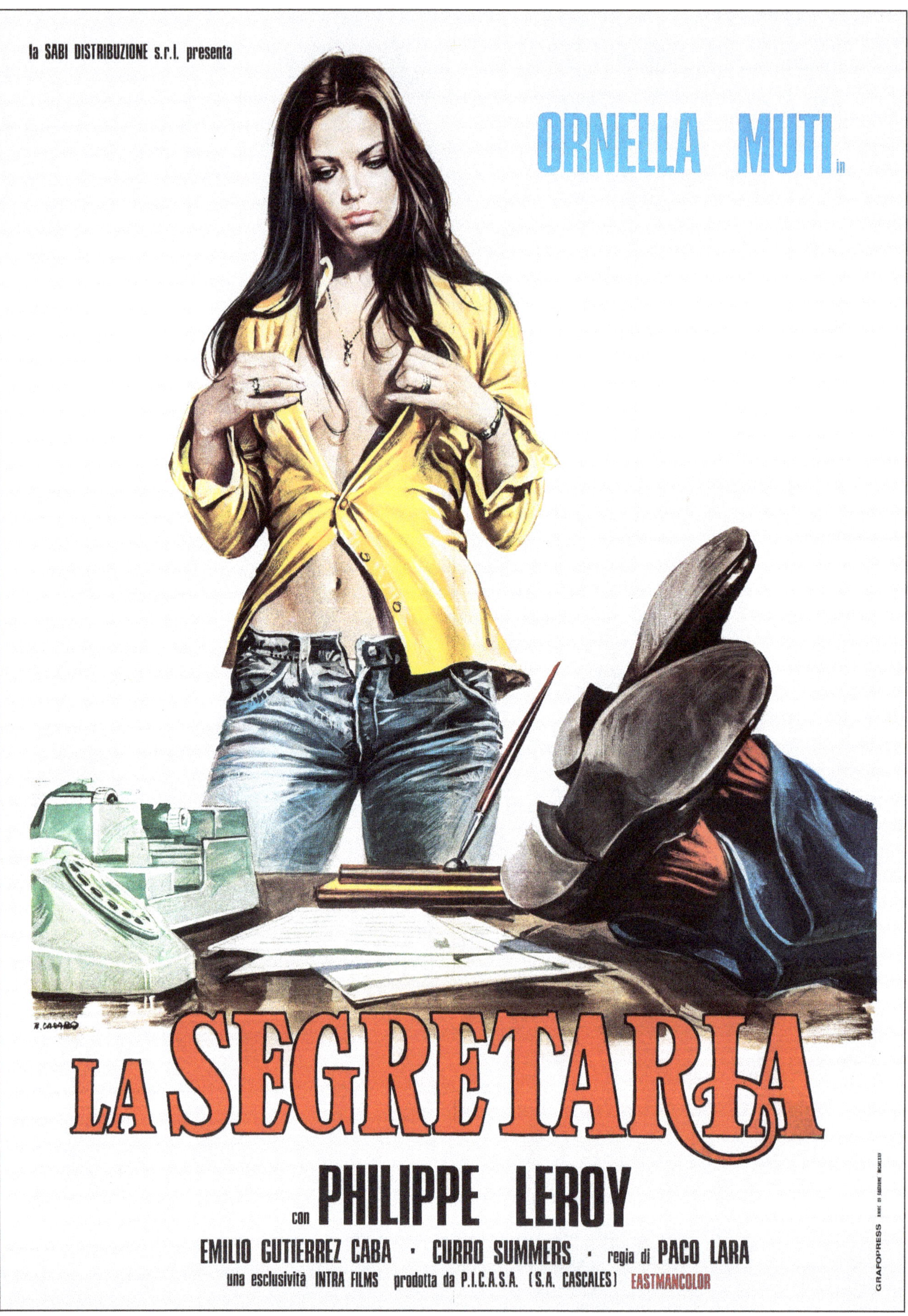

Artist: Renato Casaro. Original Title: **Cebo Para Una Adolescente** (1974).

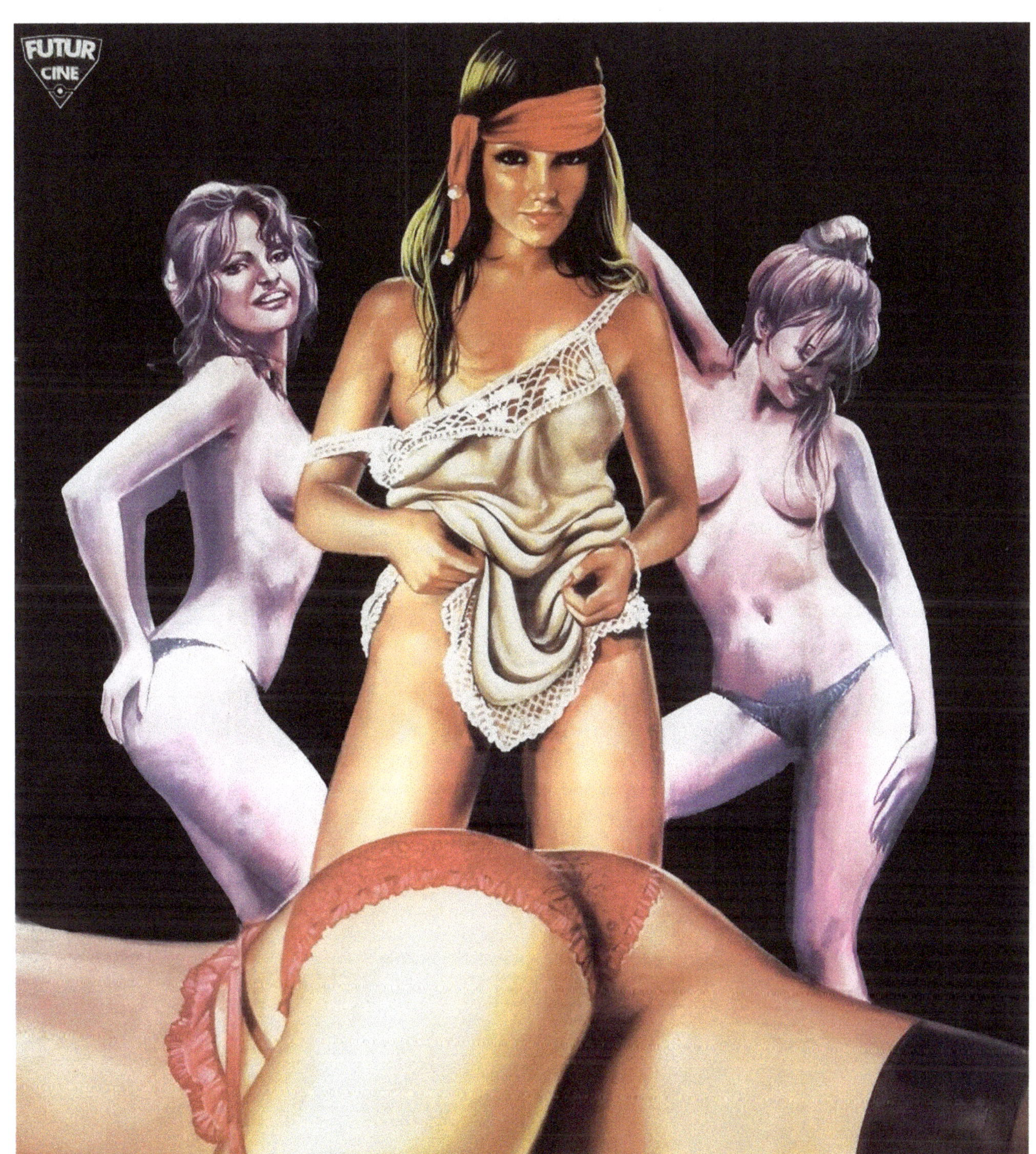

LA PORNOCAROVANA

Artist: unsigned. Original Title: **Convoi De Femmes** (1974).

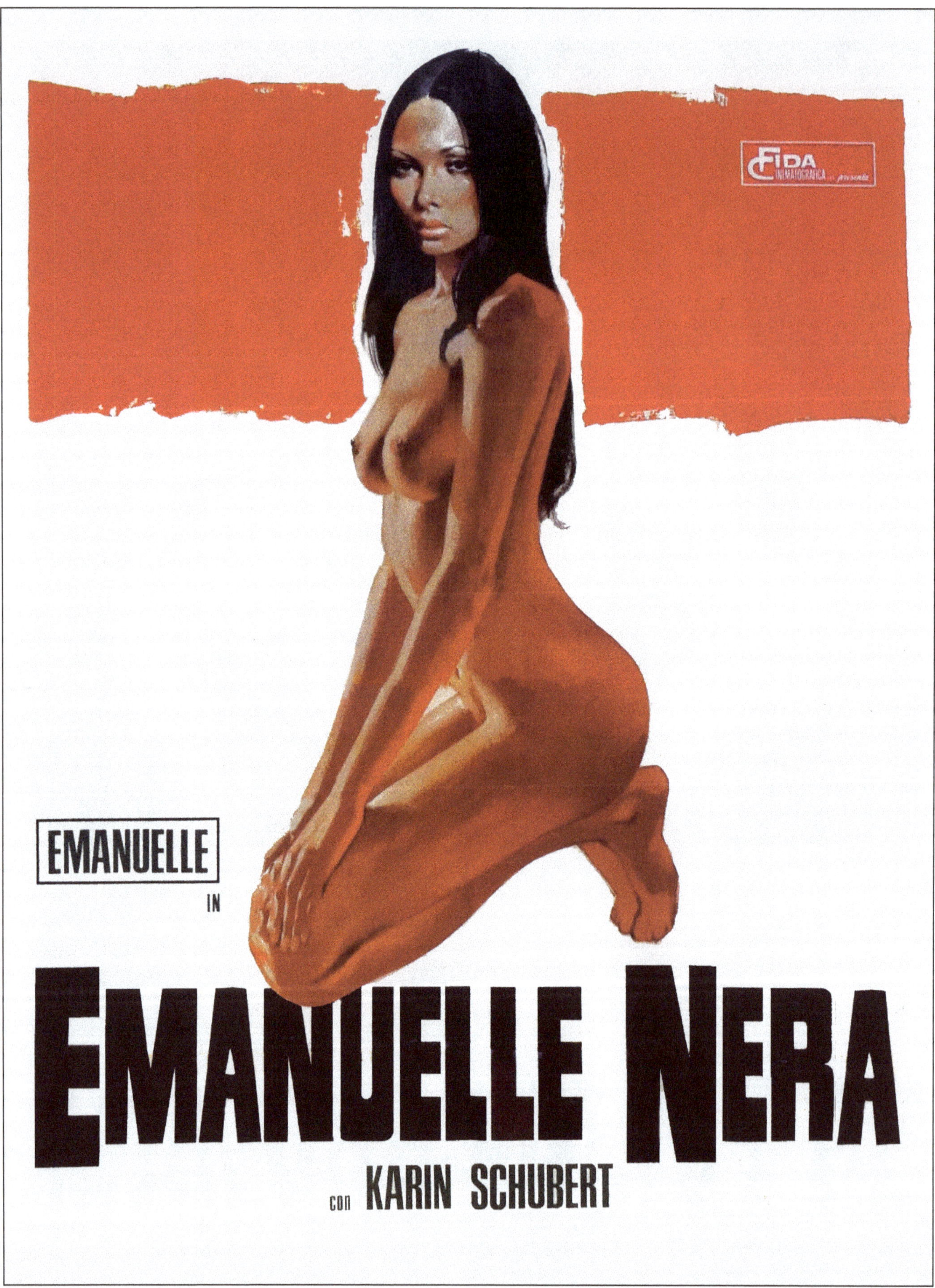

Artist: unsigned. Original Title: **Emanuelle Nera** (1975).

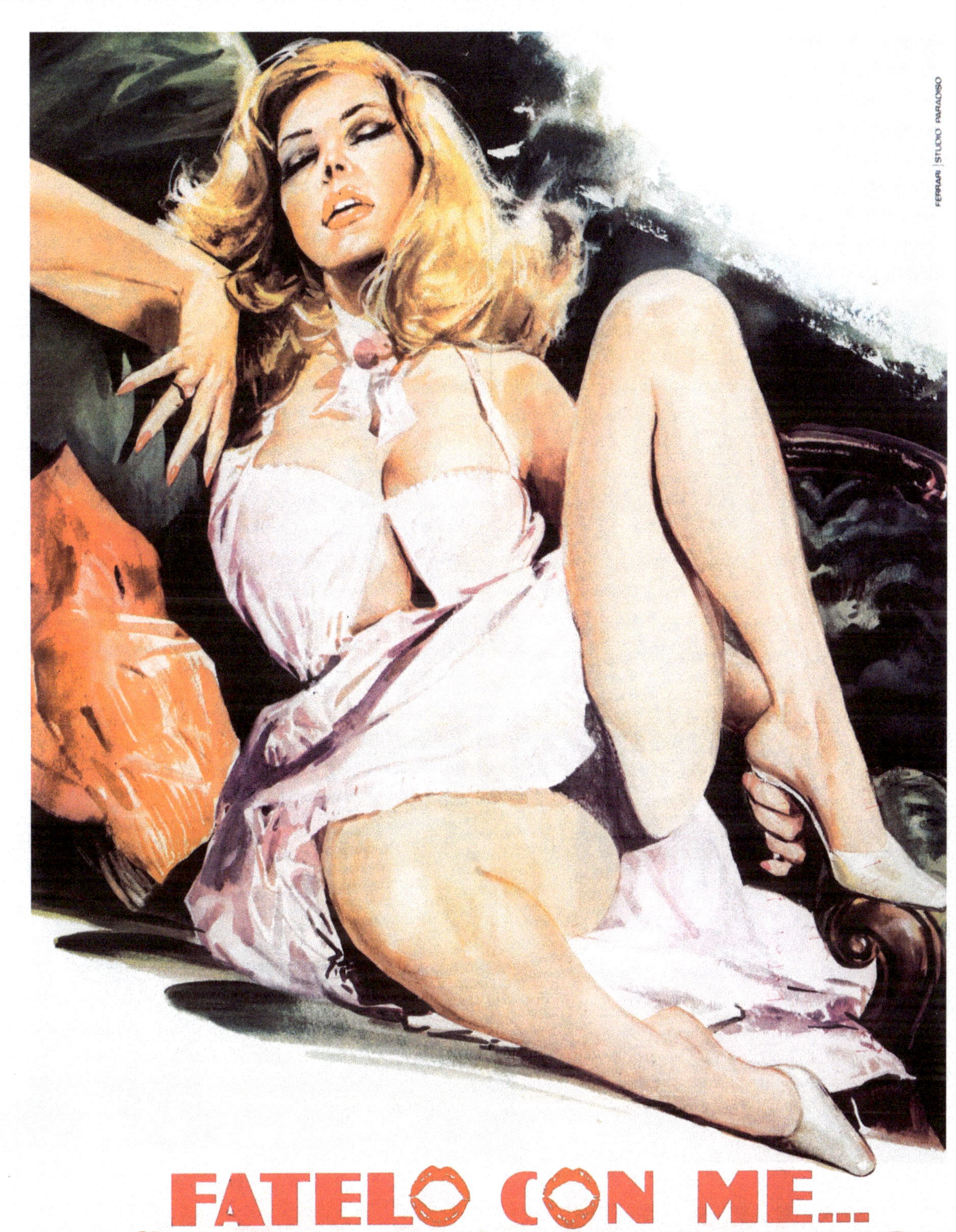

Artist: Ferrari, Studio Paradiso. Original Title: I Tyrens Tegn (1974).

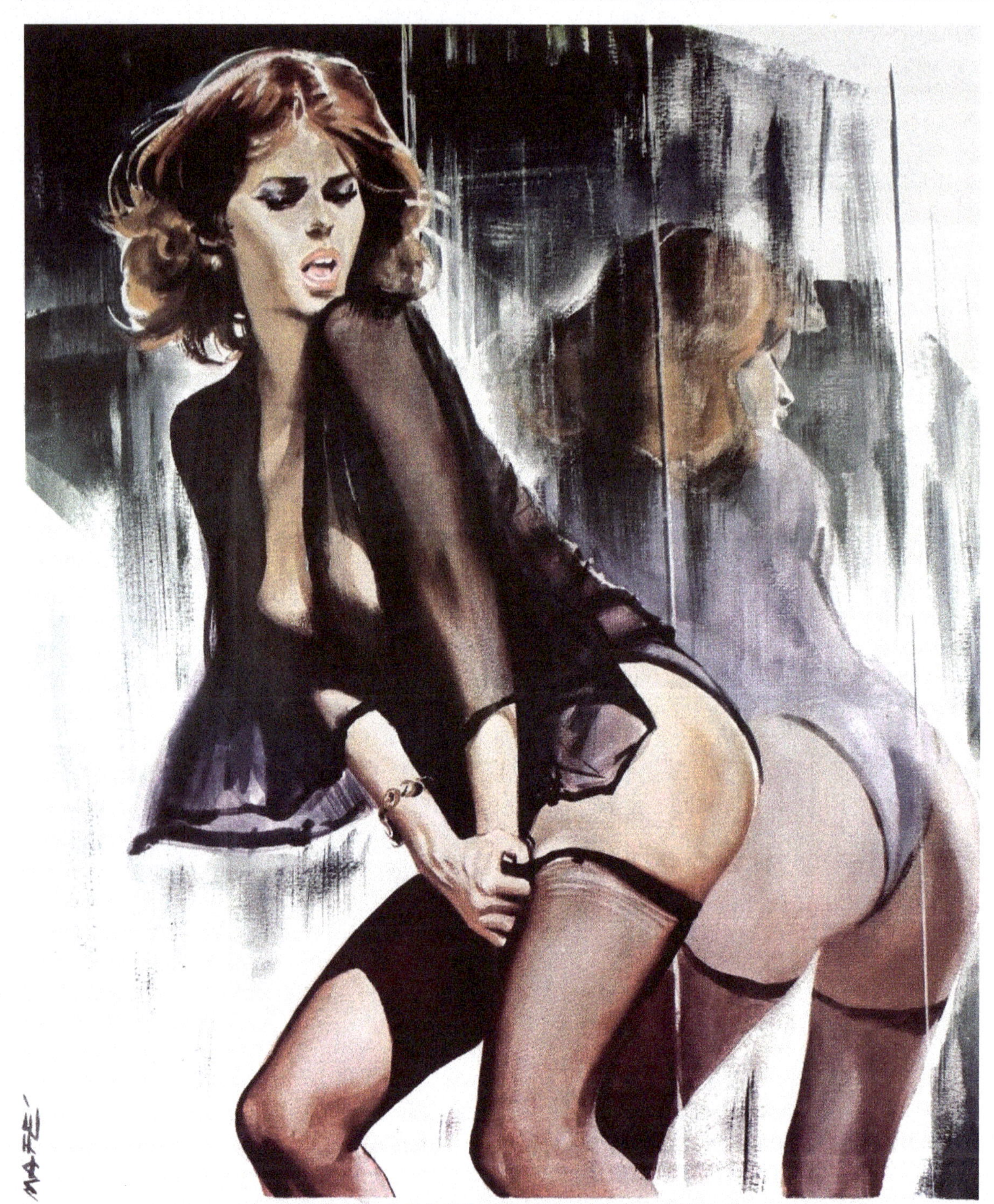

SHOCKING

Artist: Mafé. Original Title: **Shocking!** (1976).

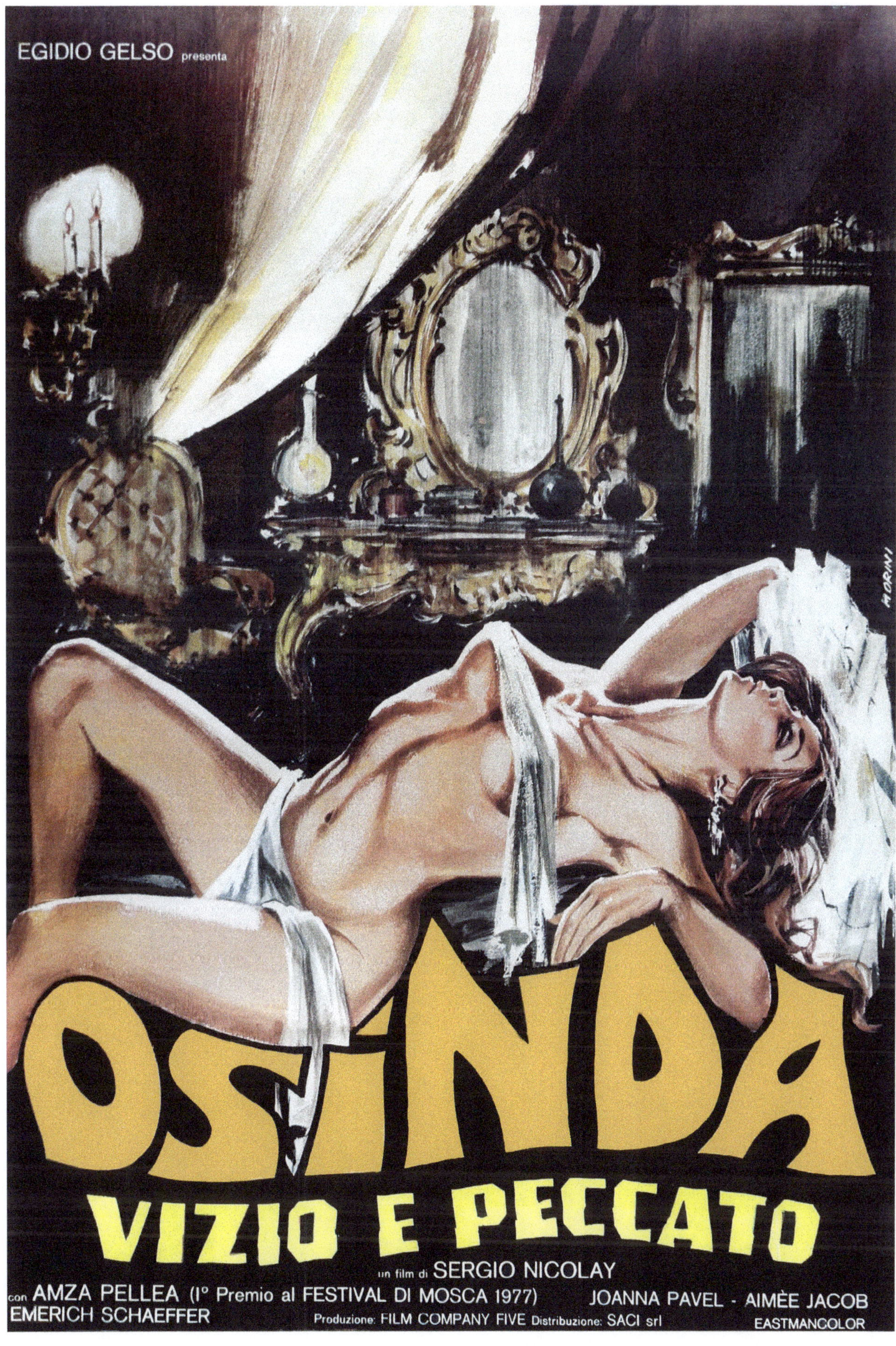

OSINDA VIZIO E PECCATO

Artist: Morini. Original Title: **Osanda** (1976).

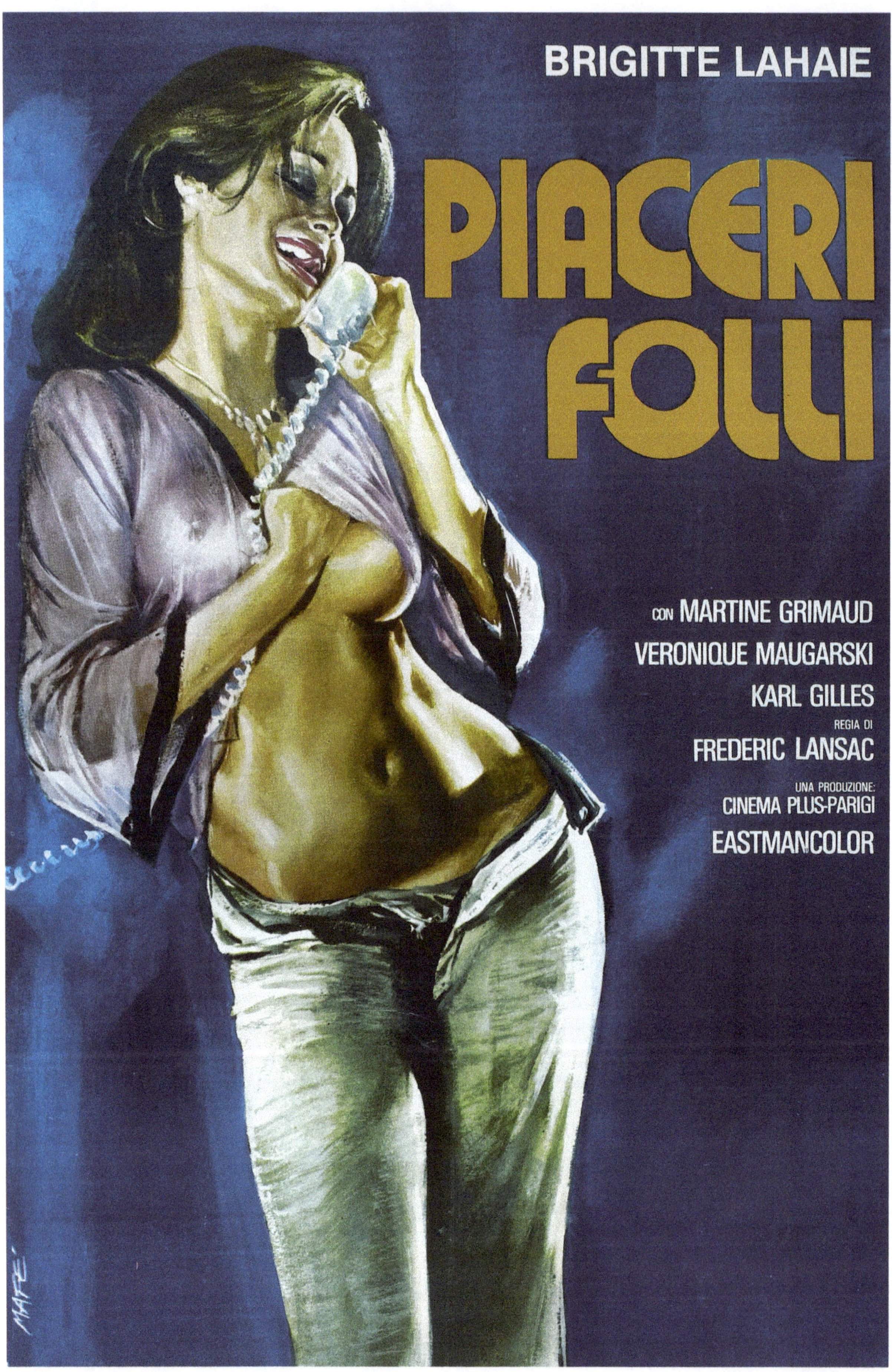

PIACERI FOLLI

Artist: Mafé. Original Title: **Mes Nuits Avec Alice, Penelope, Arnold, Maud Et Richard** (1978).

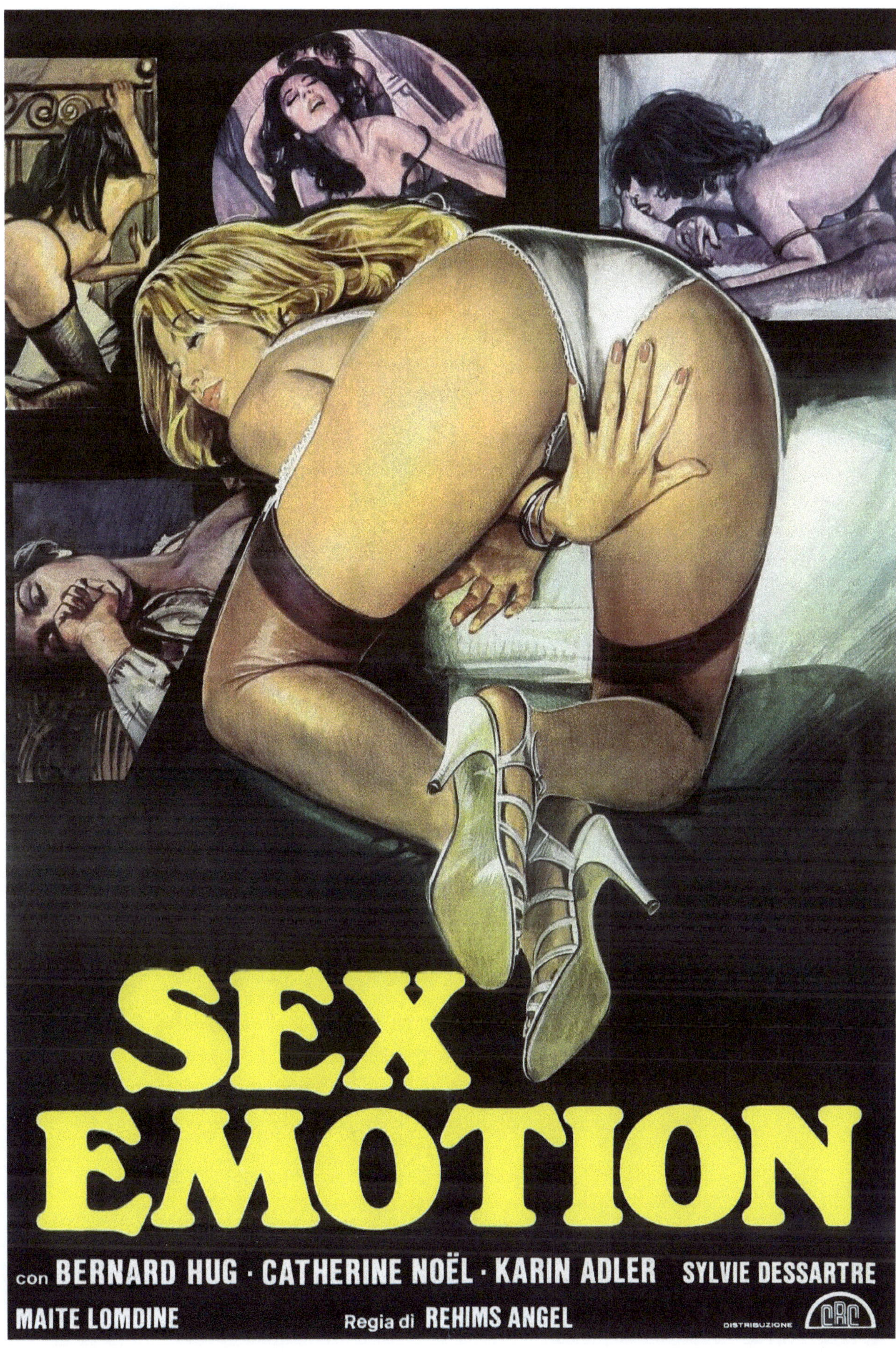

SEX
EMOTION
con BERNARD HUG · CATHERINE NOËL · KARIN ADLER   SYLVIE DESSARTRE
MAITE LOMDINE   Regia di REHIMS ANGEL
DISTRIBUZIONE CRC

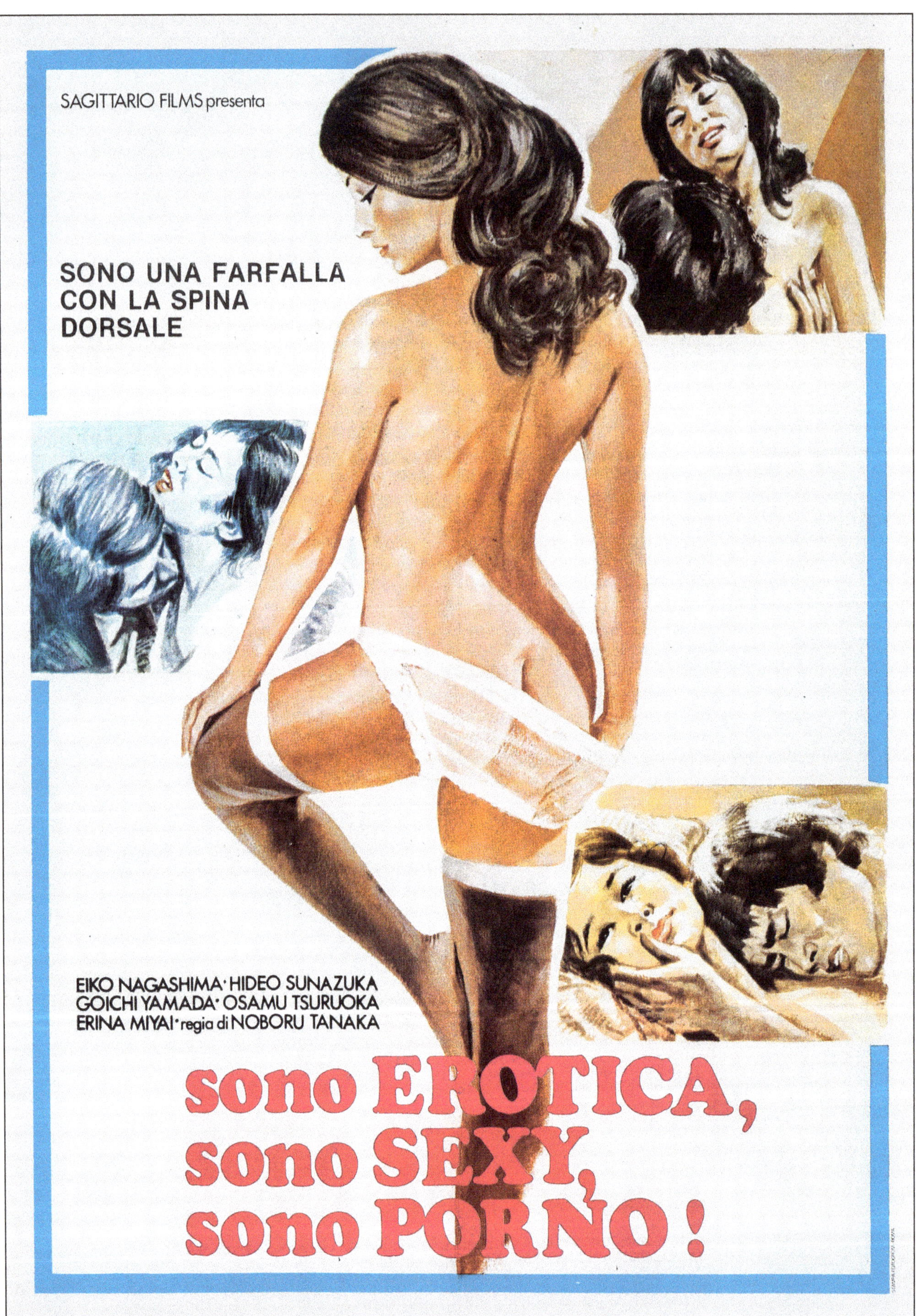

SONO EROTICA, SONO SEXY, SONO PORNO!
Artist: unsigned. Original Title: **Shiroi Hada No Karyudo: Cho No Hone** (1978).

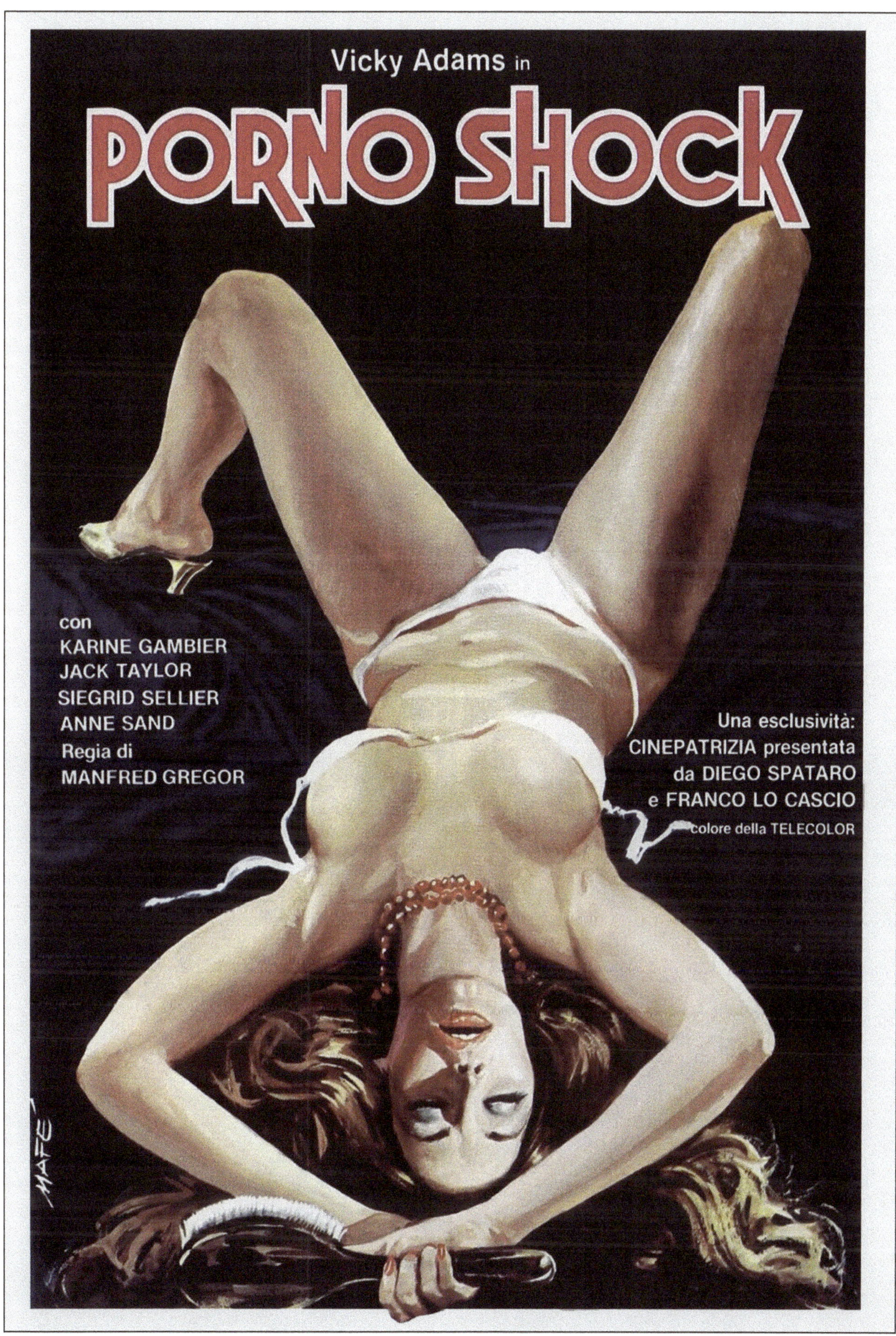

Vicky Adams in
PORNO SHOCK
con
KARINE GAMBIER
JACK TAYLOR
SIEGRID SELLIER
ANNE SAND
Regia di
MANFRED GREGOR
Una esclusività:
CINEPATRIZIA presentata
da DIEGO SPATARO
e FRANCO LO CASCIO
colore della TELECOLOR
MAFE

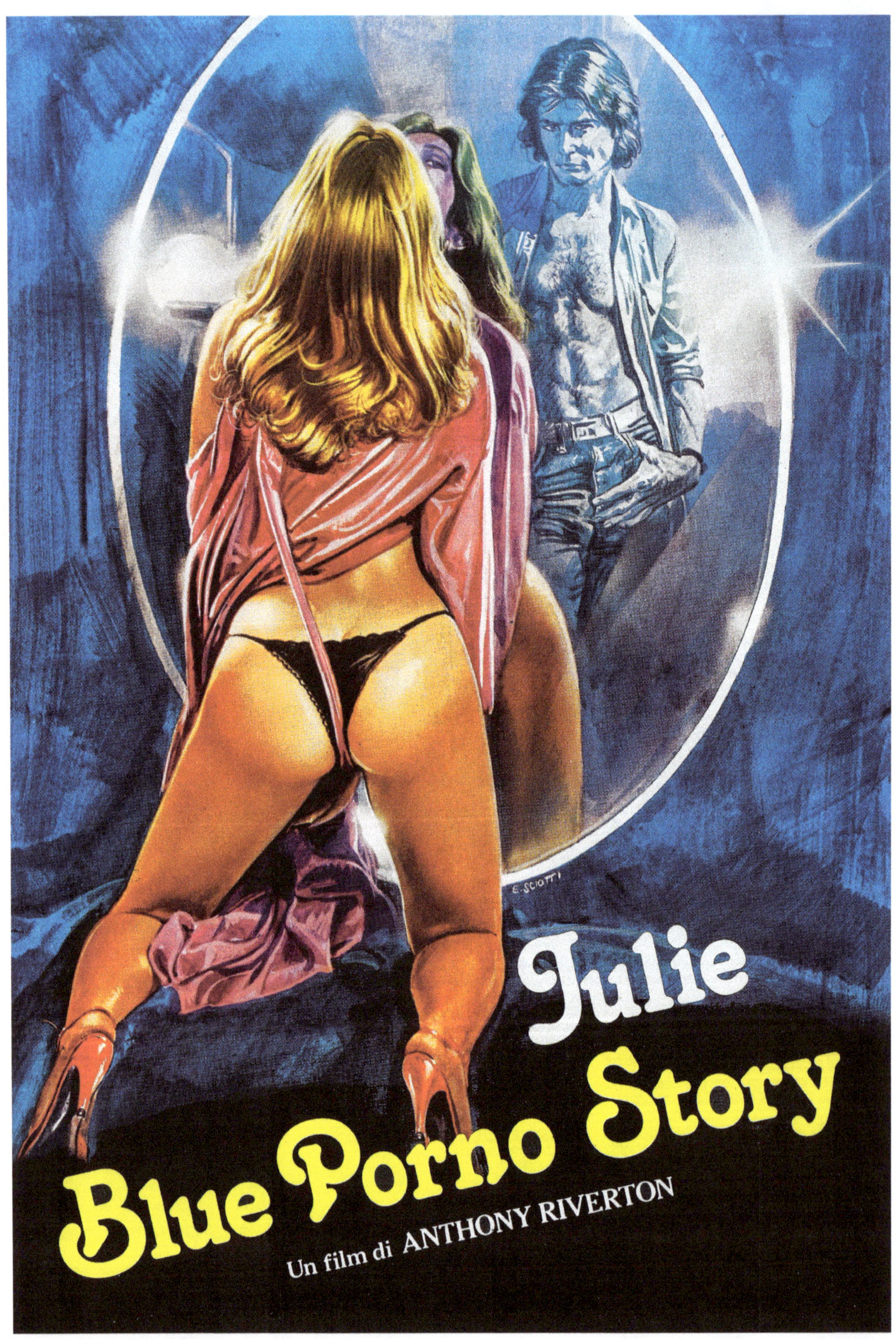

JULIE BLUE PORNO STORY
Artist: Enzo Sciotti. Original Title: The Other Side Of Julie (1978)

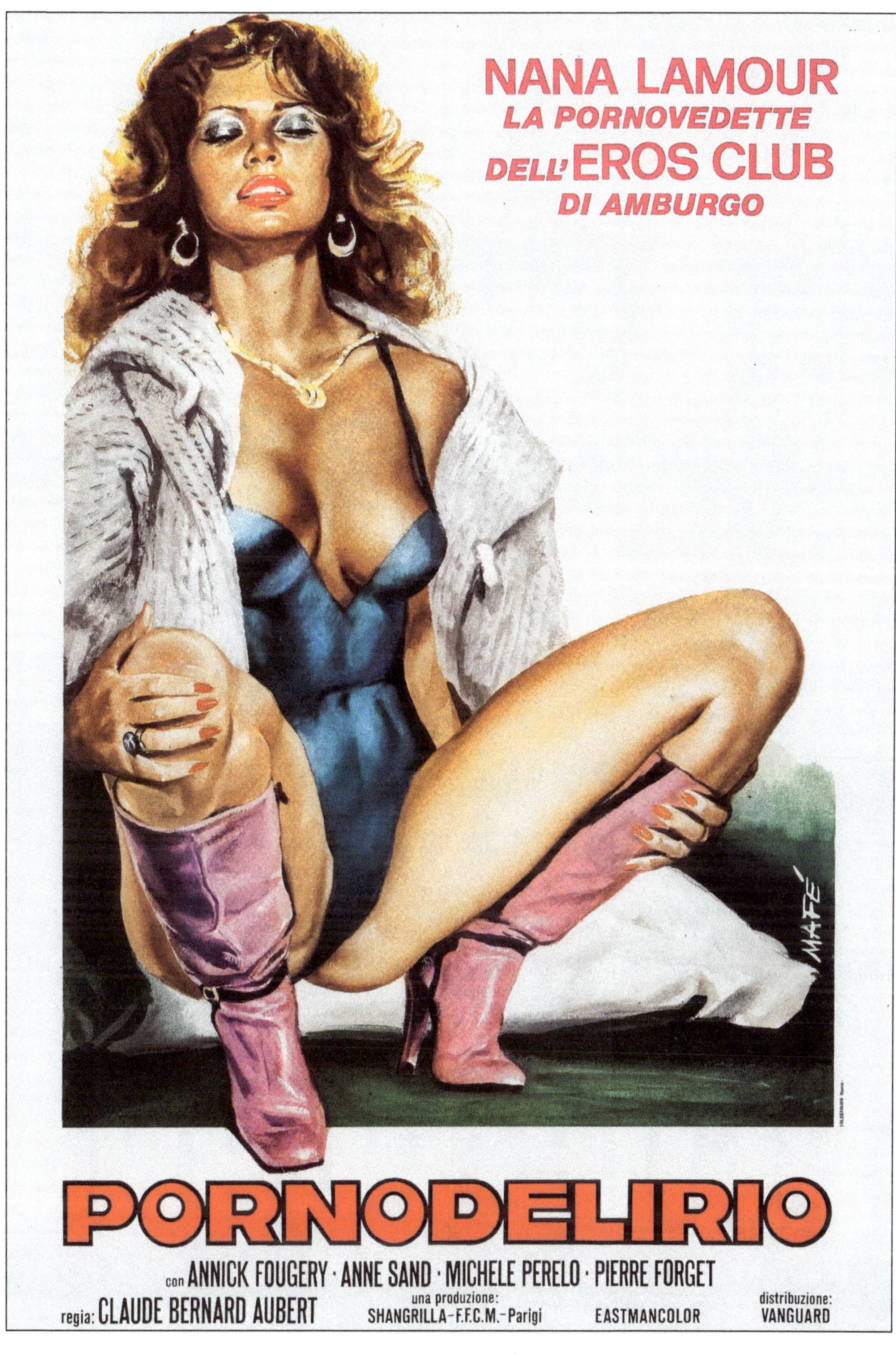

NANA LAMOUR
LA PORNOVEDETTE
DELL'EROS CLUB
DI AMBURGO
MAFÉ
PORNODELIRIO
con ANNICK FOUGERY · ANNE SAND · MICHELE PERELO · PIERRE FORGET
regia: CLAUDE BERNARD AUBERT
una produzione:
SHANGRILLA–F.F.C.M.–Parigi
EASTMANCOLOR
distribuzione:
VANGUARD

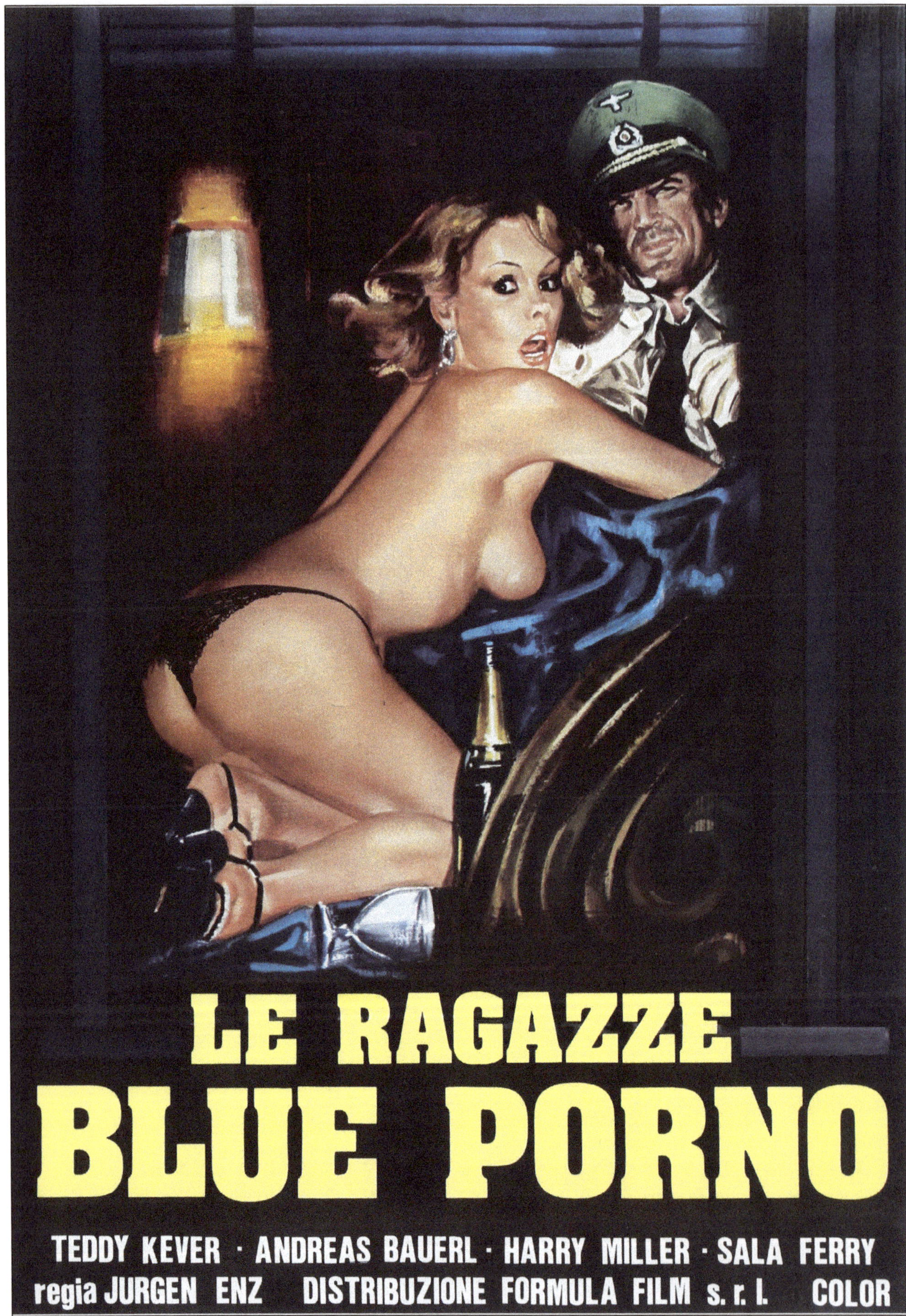

LE RAGAZZE BLUE PORNO

Artist: unsigned. Original Title: **Die Neuen Abenteuer Des Sanitatsgefreiten Neumann (1978).**

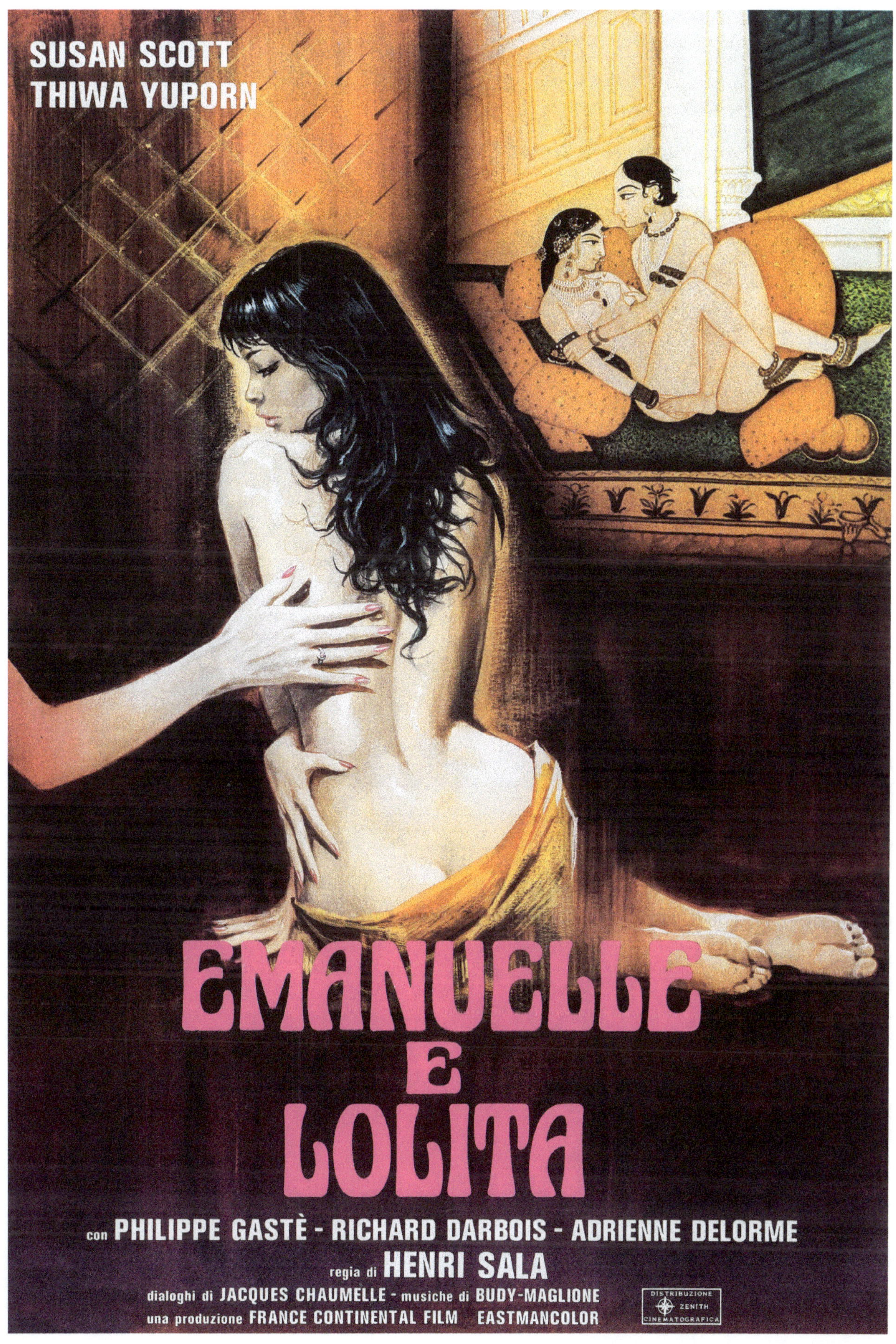

Artist: unsigned. Original Title: **Emanuelle E Lolita** (1978).

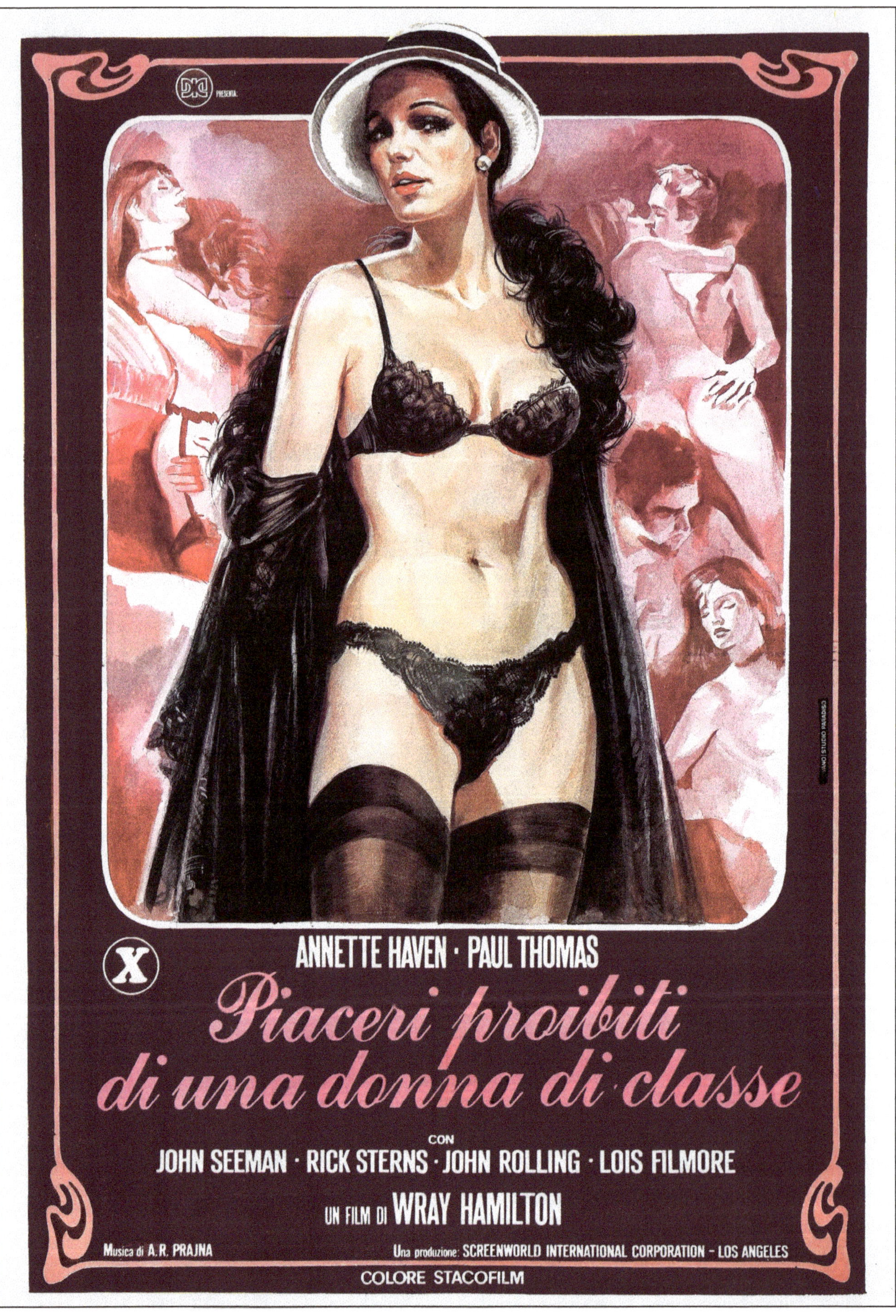

PIACERI PROIBITI DI UNA DONNA DI CLASSE

Artist: Mario Piovano (Studio Paradiso). Original Title: **Soft Places** (1978).

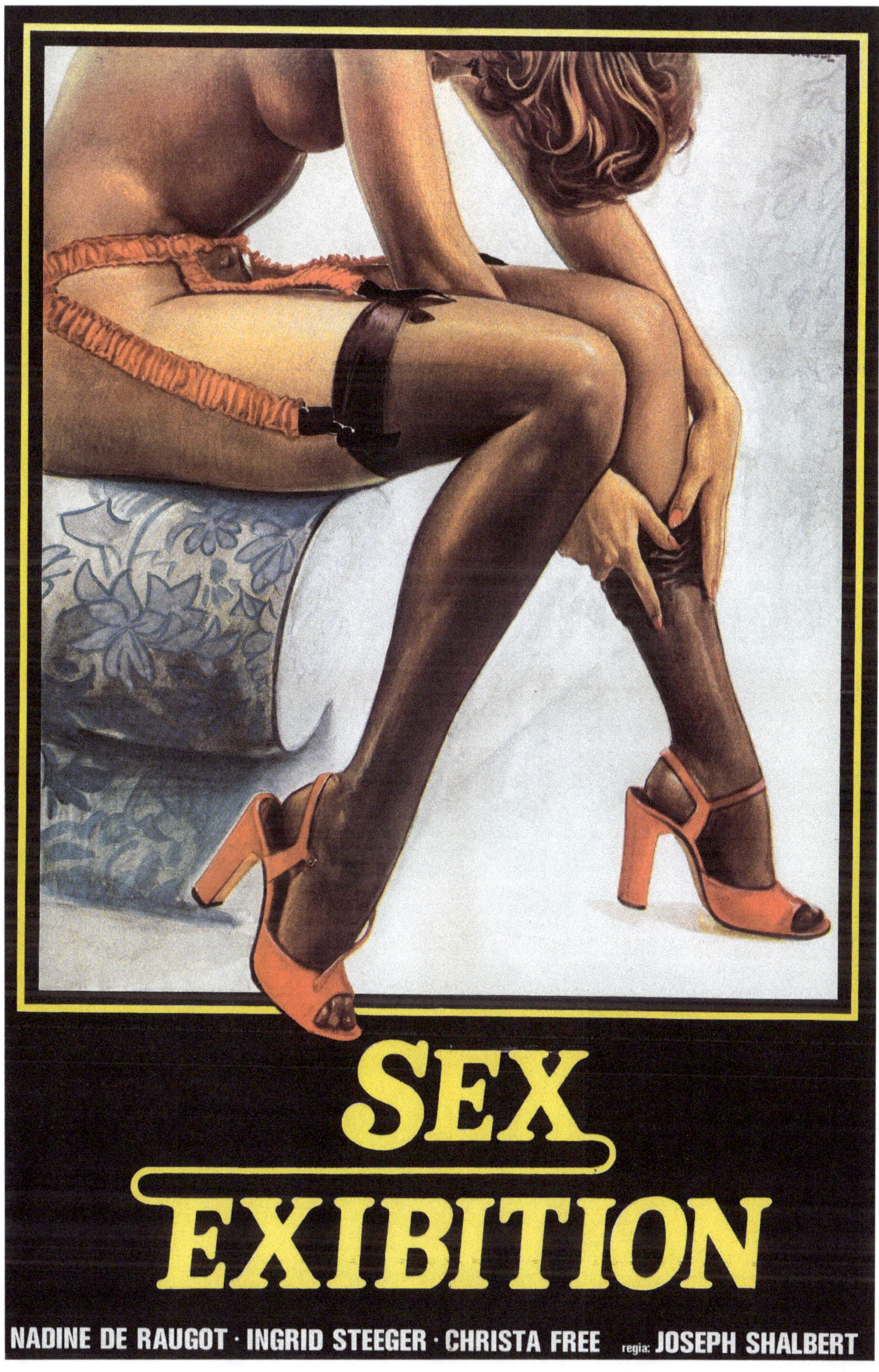

Artist: Enzo Sciotti. Original Title: **Madchen Wie Am Wege Liegen** (1978).

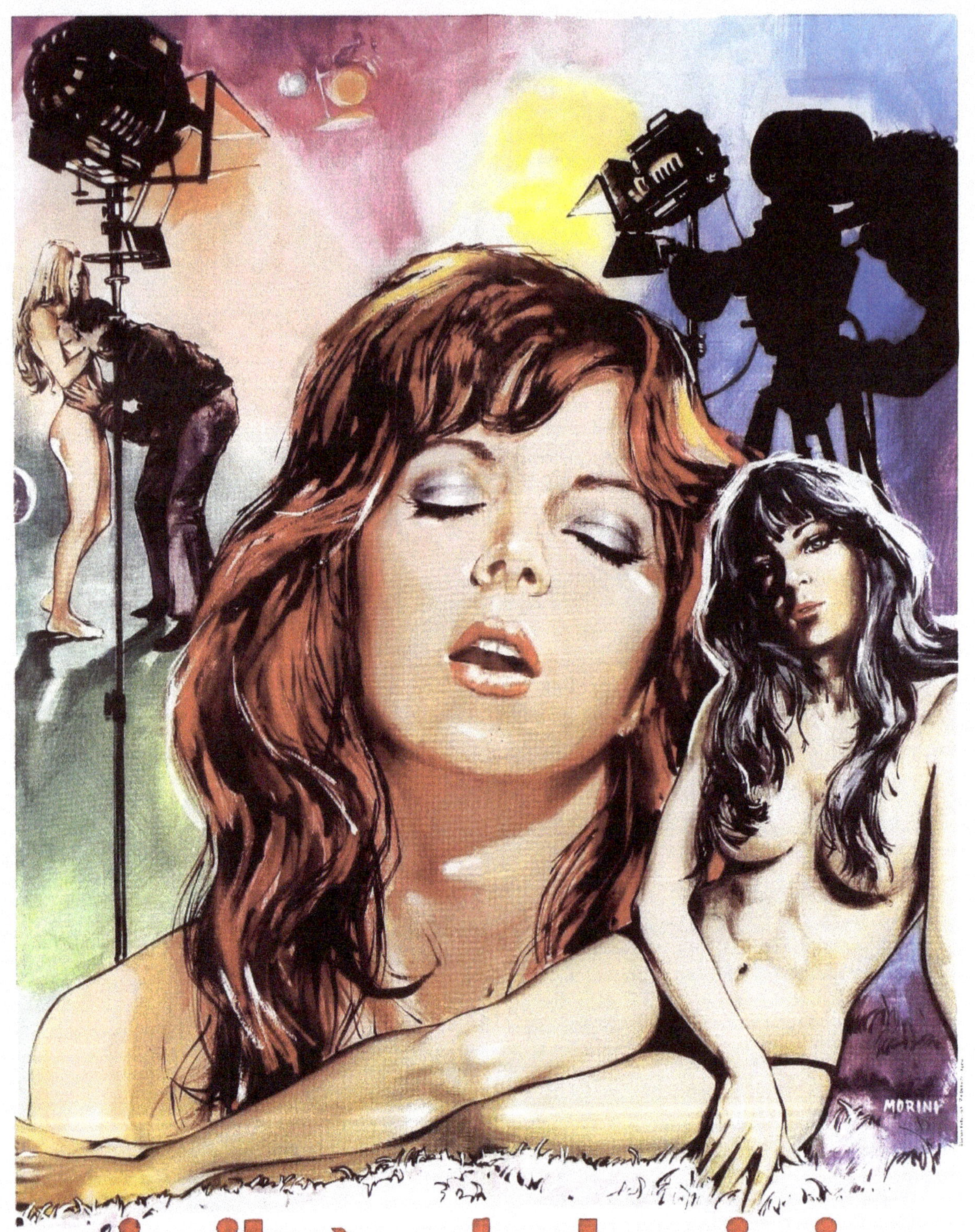

CIVILTA DEL VIZIO

Artist: Morini. Original Title: **Confessions Of A Blue Movie Star** (1978).

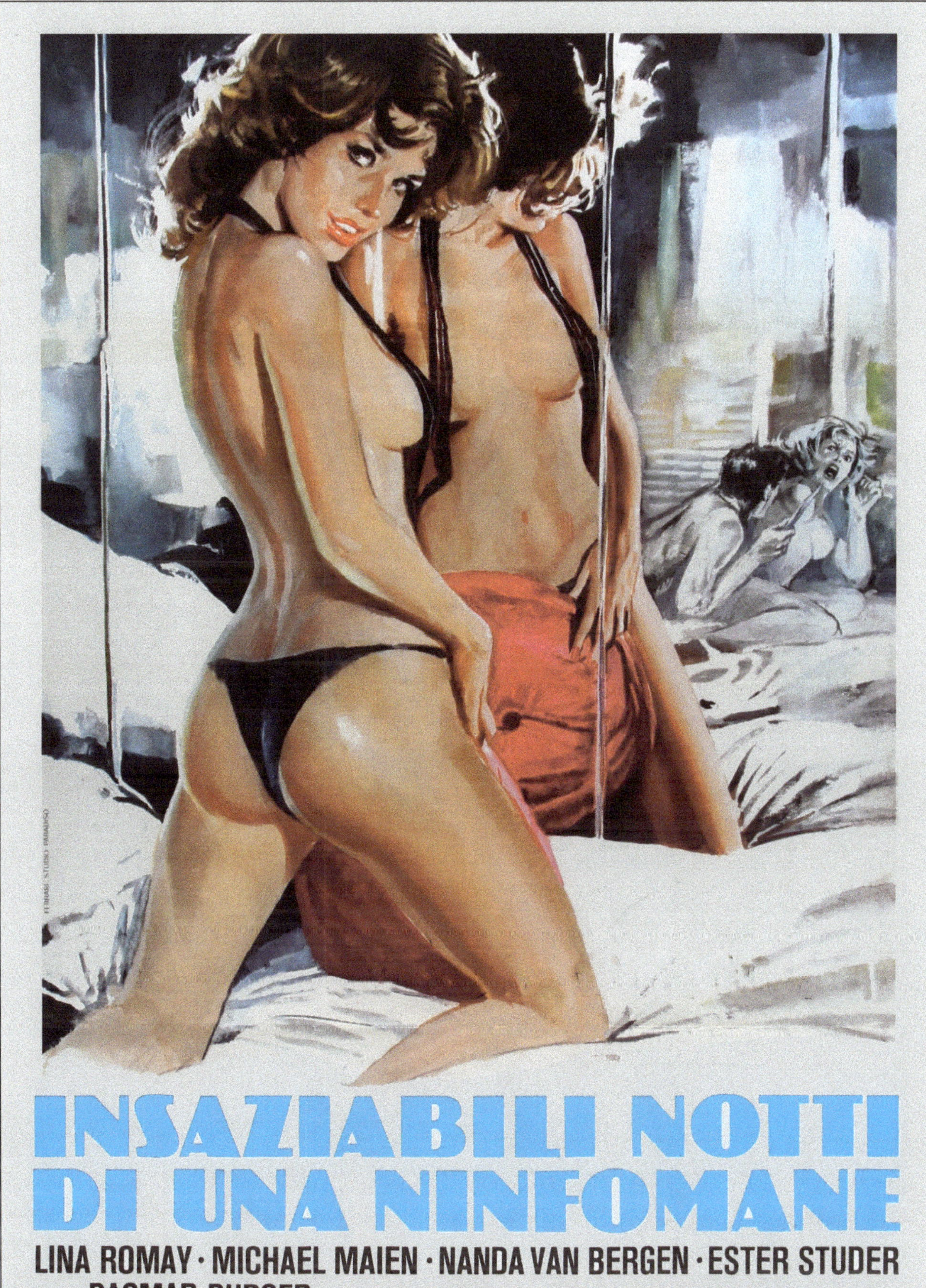

Artist: Ferrari (Studio Paradiso). Original Title: **Frauen Ohne Unschuld** (1978).

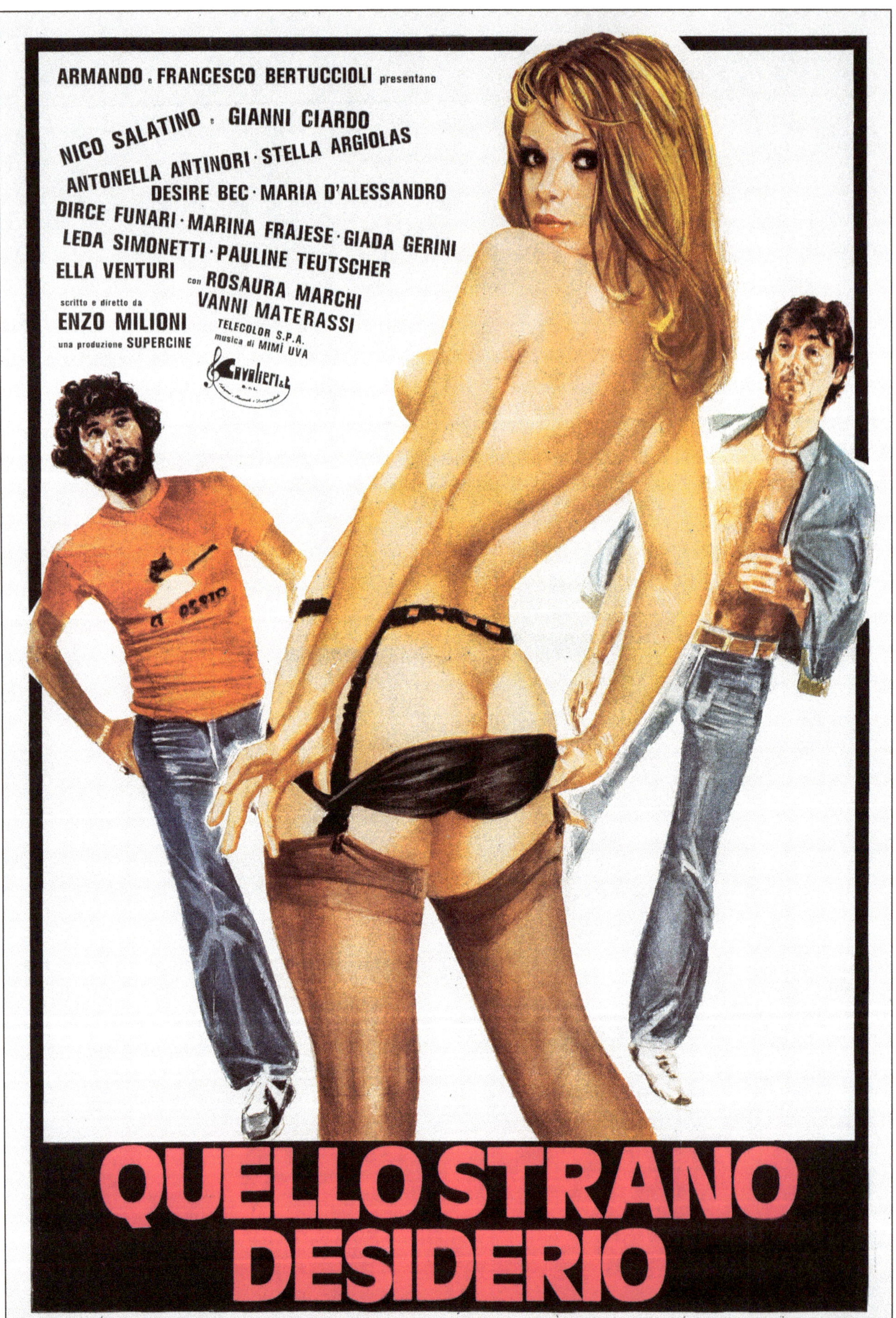
ARMANDO e FRANCESCO BERTUCCIOLI presentano
NICO SALATINO e GIANNI CIARDO
ANTONELLA ANTINORI · STELLA ARGIOLAS
DESIRE BEC · MARIA D'ALESSANDRO
DIRCE FUNARI · MARINA FRAJESE · GIADA GERINI
LEDA SIMONETTI · PAULINE TEUTSCHER
ELLA VENTURI con ROSAURA MARCHI
VANNI MATERASSI
scritto e diretto da
ENZO MILIONI
una produzione SUPERCINE
TELECOLOR S.P.A.
musica di MIMÌ UVA
QUELLO STRANO
DESIDERIO

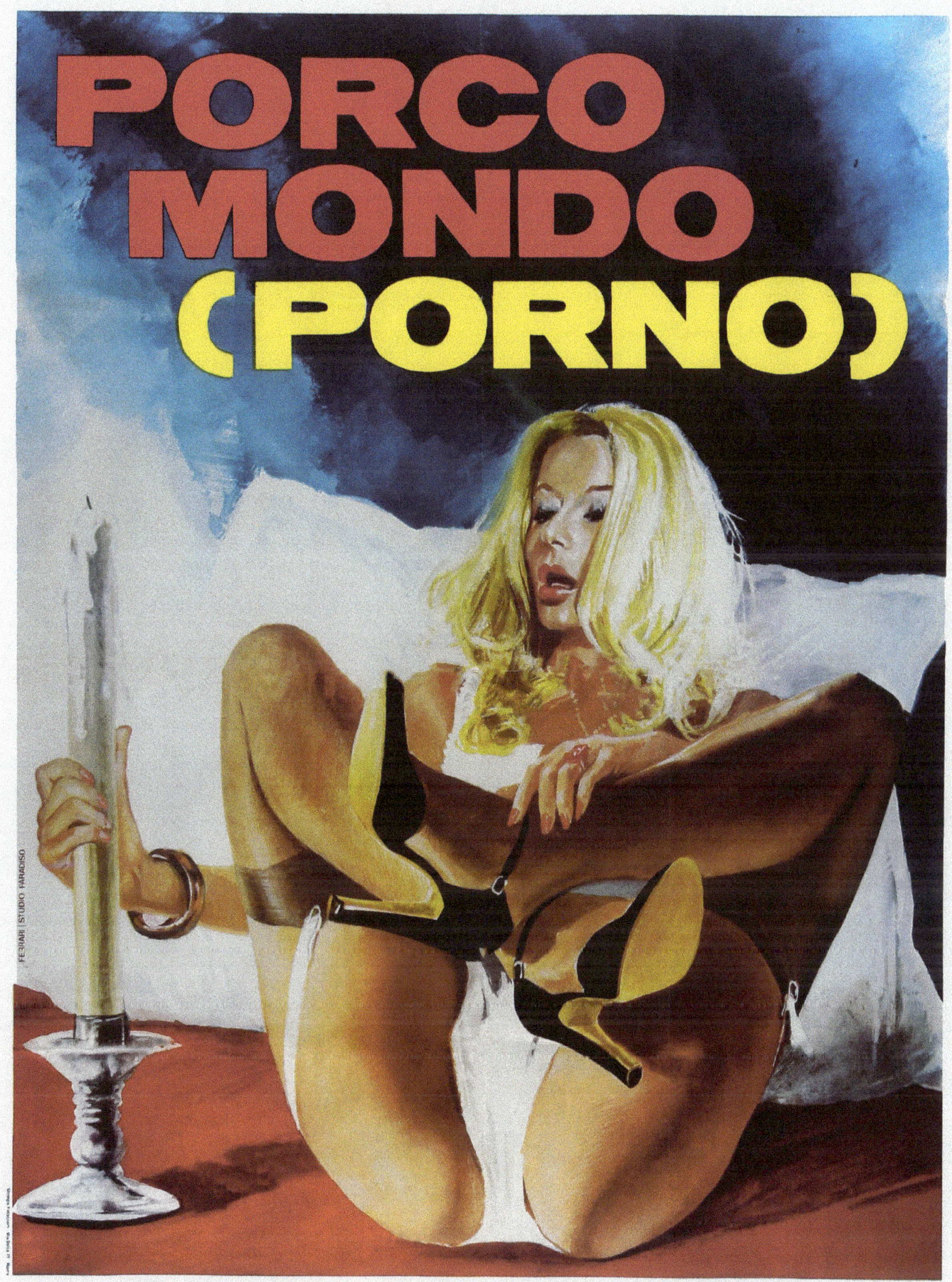

KARIN WELL in
PORCO MONDO (PORNO)
FERRARI (STUDIO PARADISO)
con CARLO DE MEJO - BARBARA REY con ARTHUR KENNEDY
e con ALIDA VALLA   un film di SERGIO BERGONZELLI
EASTMANCOLOR CINEMASCOPE
PBC

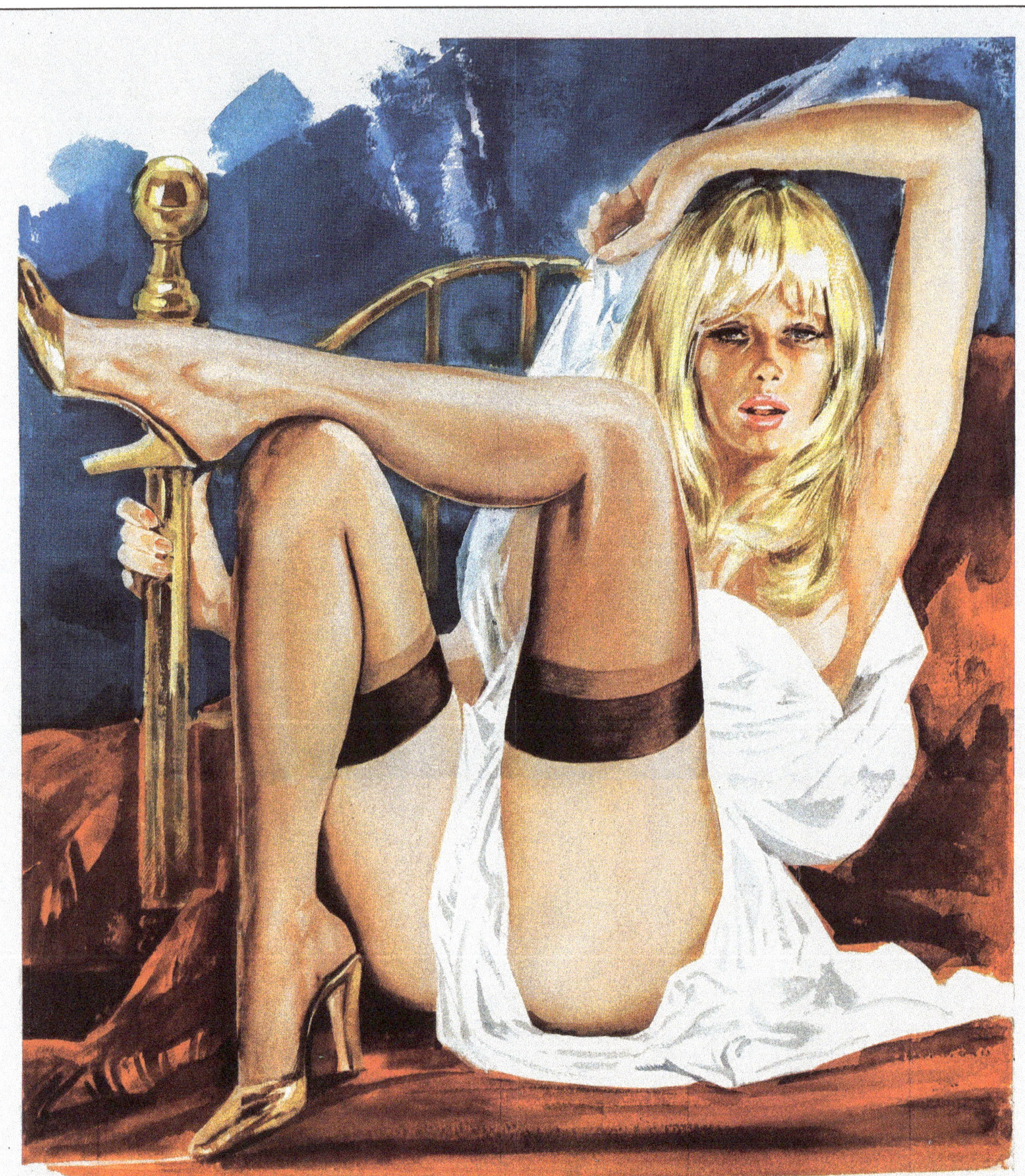

TORBIDI DESIDERI DI UNA NINFOMANE

Artist: unsigned. Original Title: **Tokyo Emmanuelle Fujin** (1975).

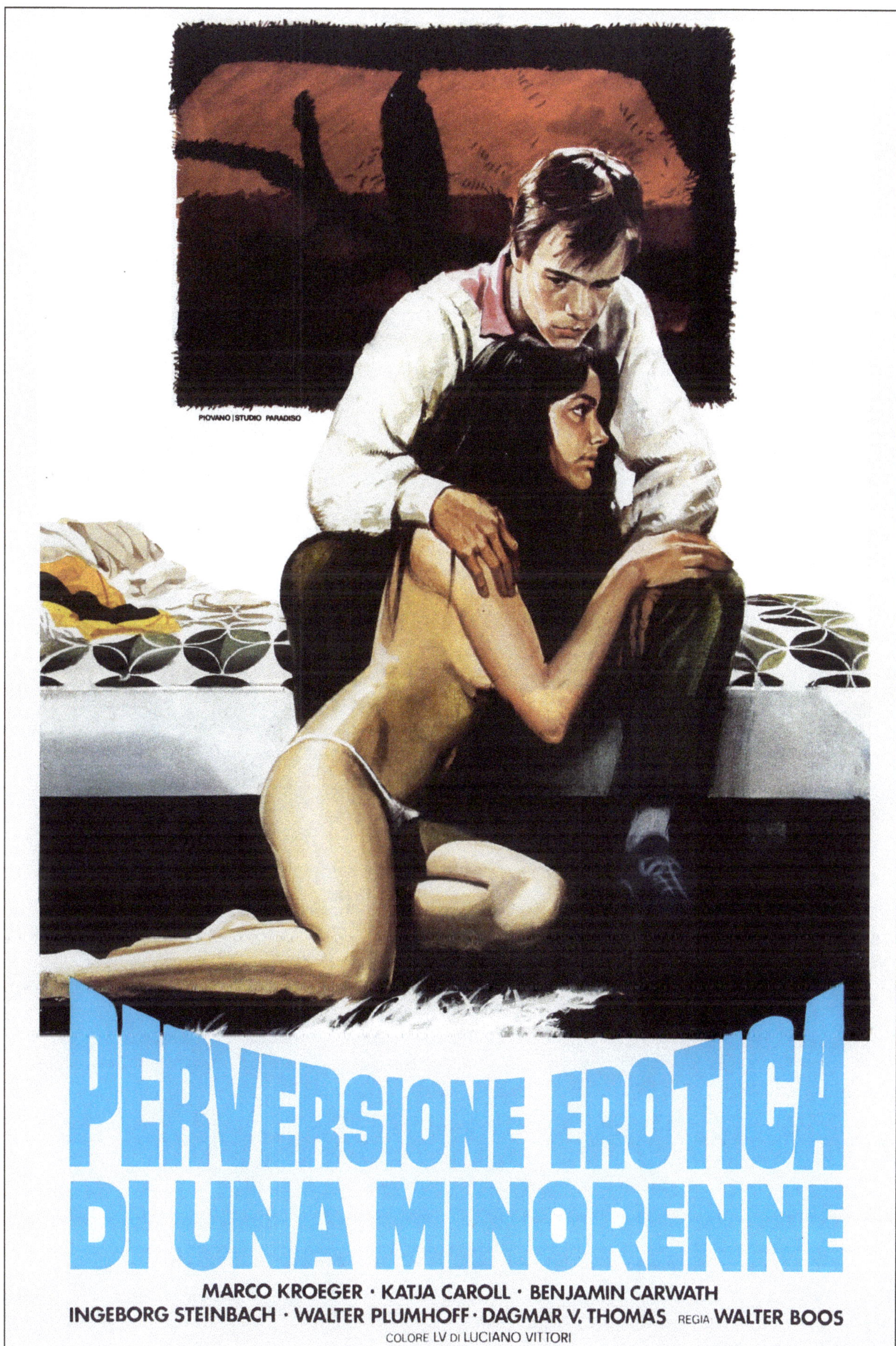

Artist: Mario Piovano (Studio Paradiso). Original Title: **Die Schulmadchen Vom Treffpunkt Zoo (1979)**.

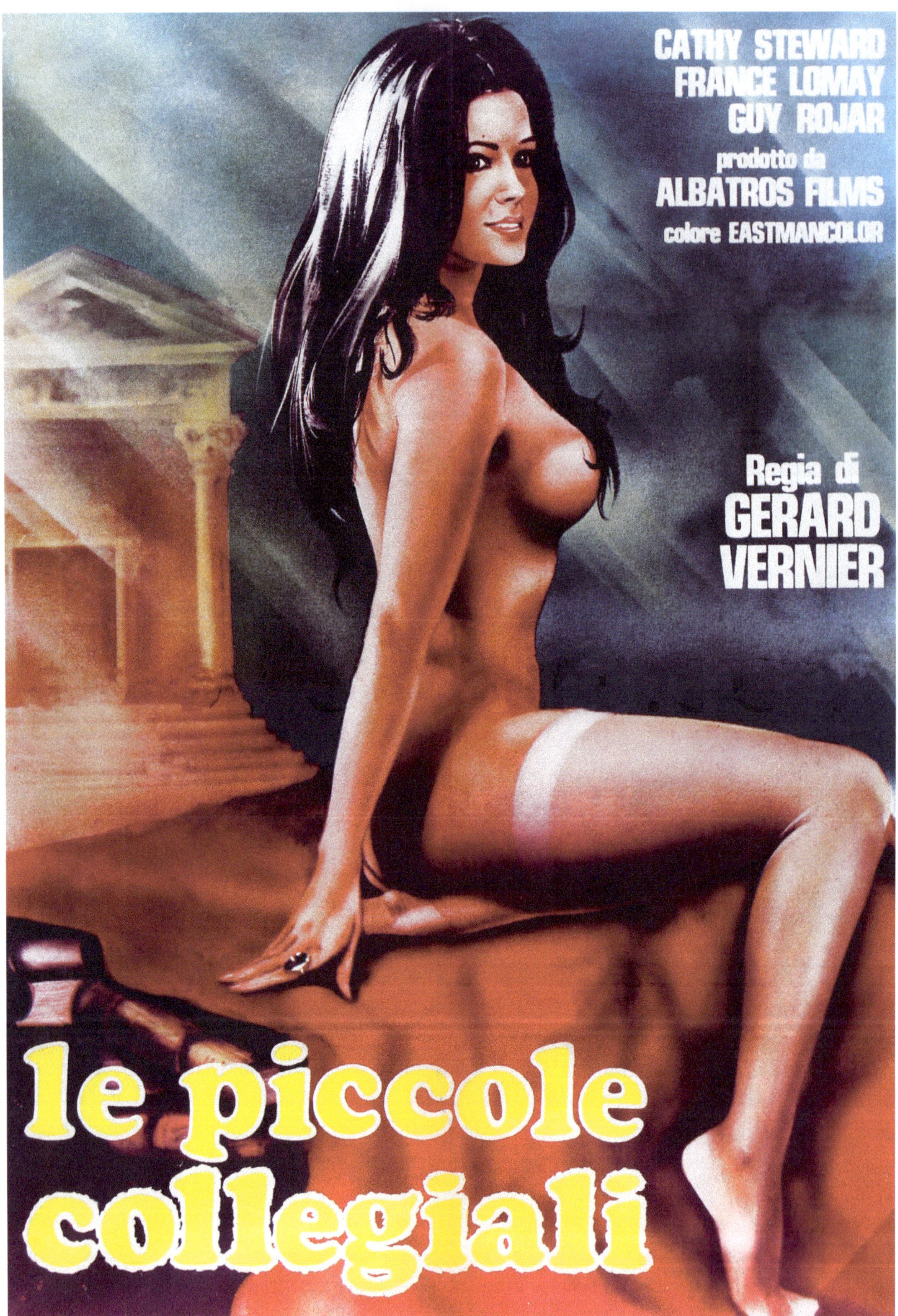

Artist: unsigned. Original Title: **Hôtesses En Chaleur** (1979).

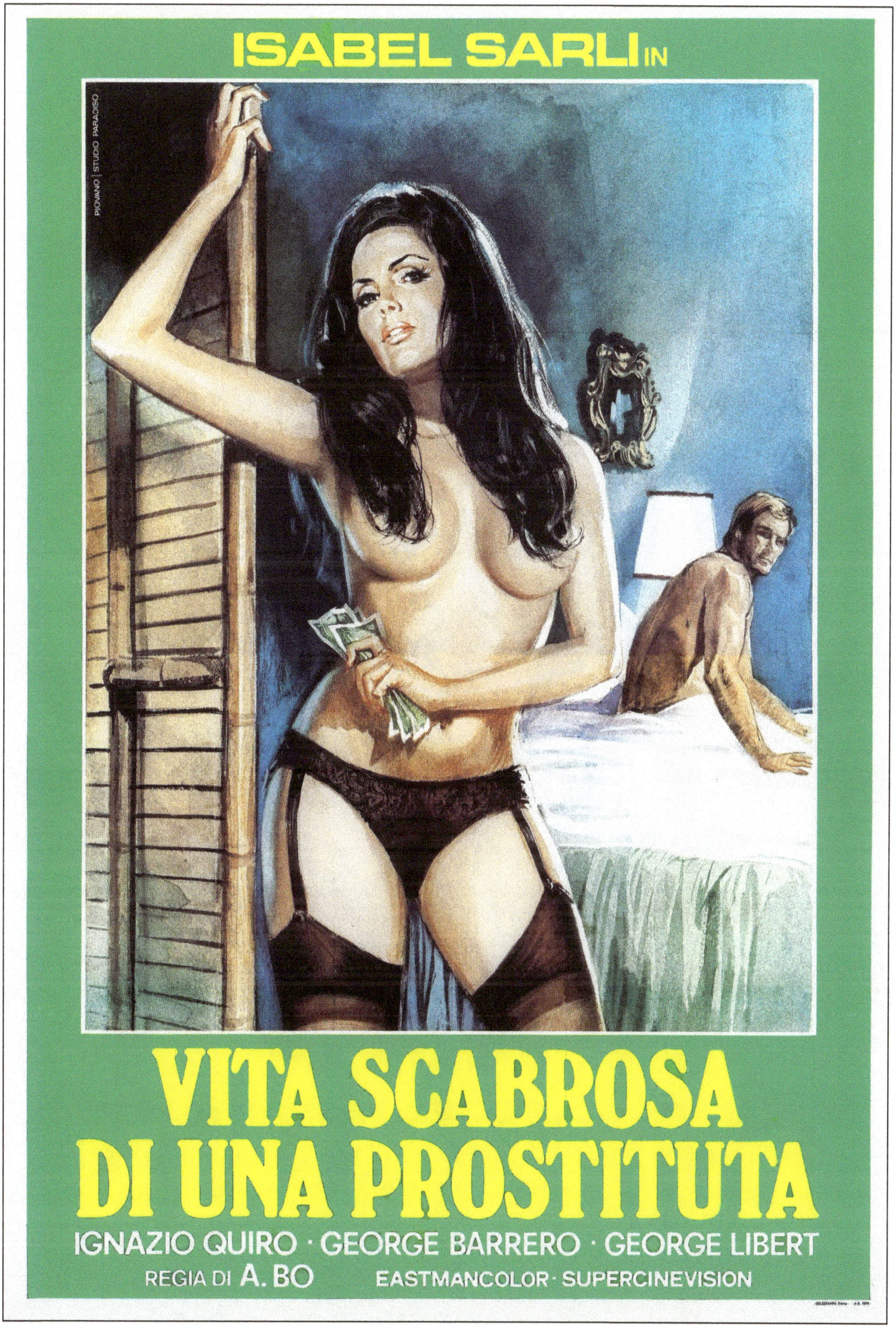

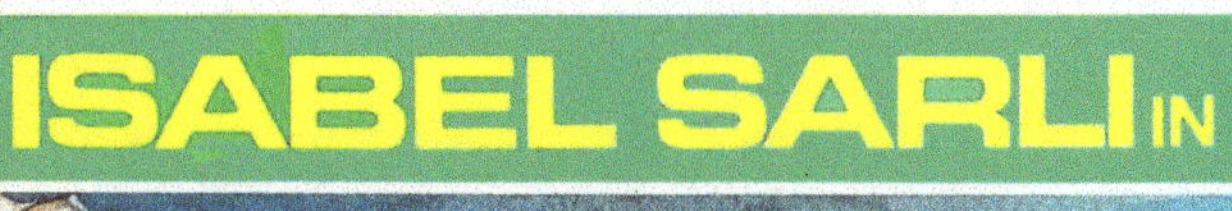

Artist: Mario Piovano (Studio Paradiso). Original Title: **El Sexo Y El Amor** (1974).

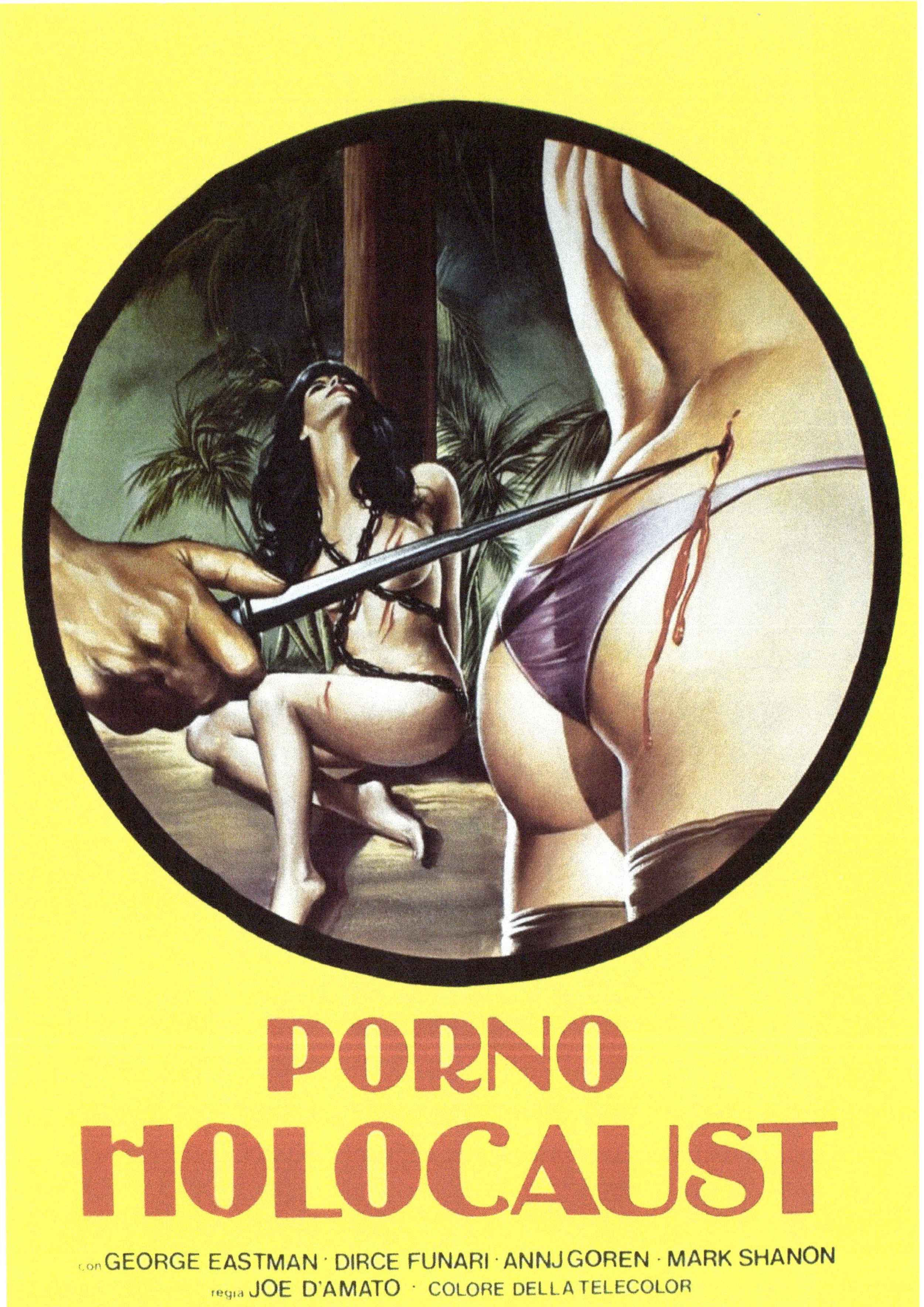

PORNO HOLOCAUST

Artist: unsigned. Original Title: **Porno Holocaust** (1981).

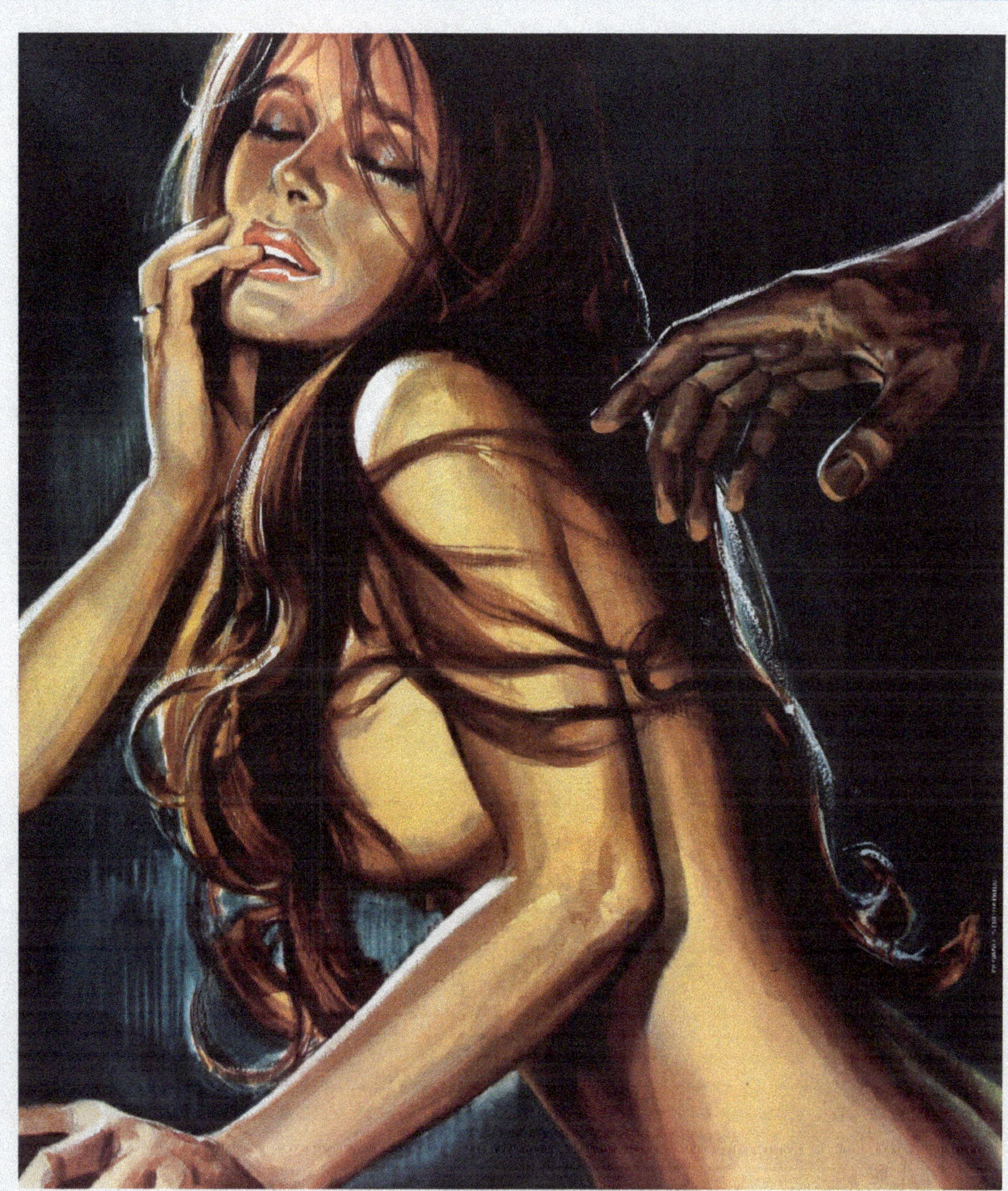

Artist: Mario Piovano (Studio Paradiso). Original Title: **Partouzes** (1980).

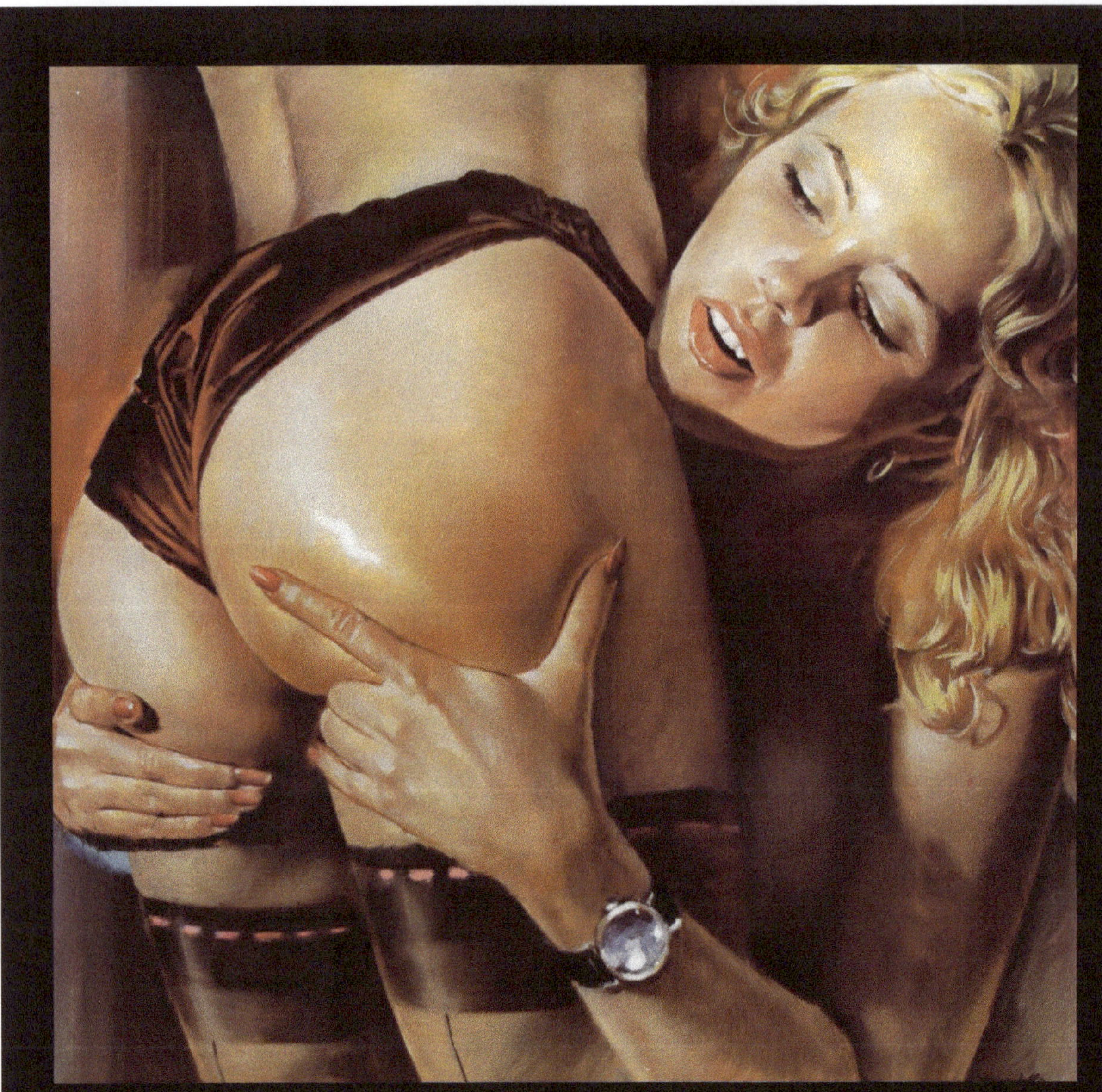

FOLLI PIACERI DELLE PORNO PRIGIONIERE

Artist: unsigned. Original Title: **Gegangene Frauen** (1980).

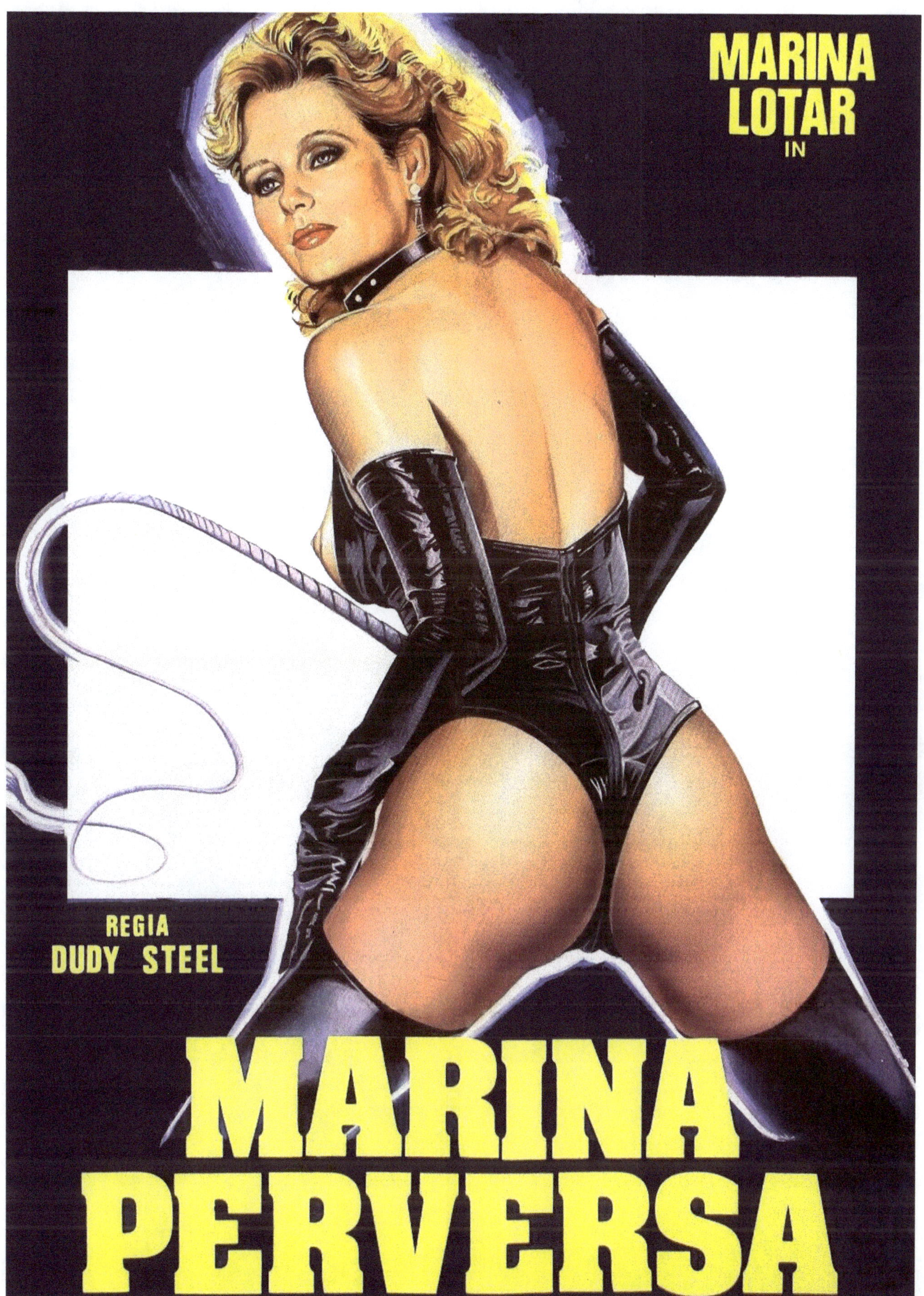

MARINA
LOTAR
IN
REGIA
DUDY STEEL
MARINA
PERVERSA

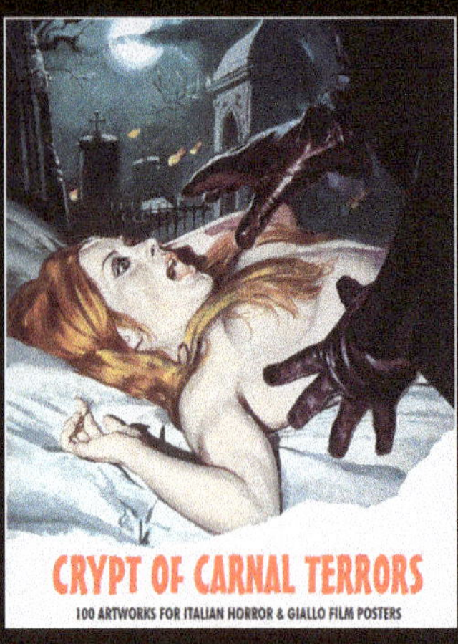
CRYPT OF CARNAL TERRORS
100 ARTWORKS FOR ITALIAN HORROR & GIALLO FILM POSTERS

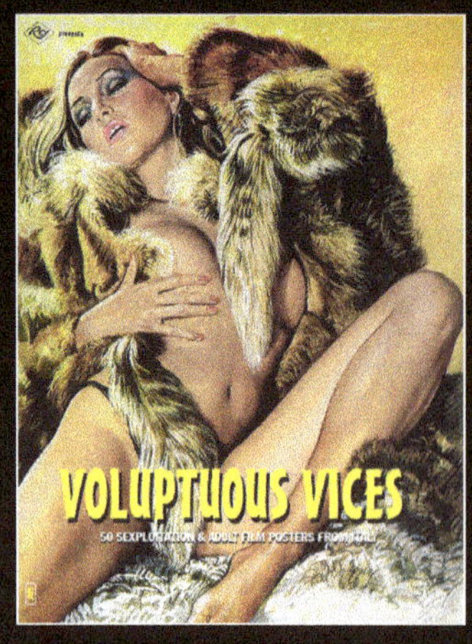
VOLUPTUOUS VICES
50 SEXPLOITATION & ADULT FILM POSTERS FROM ITALY

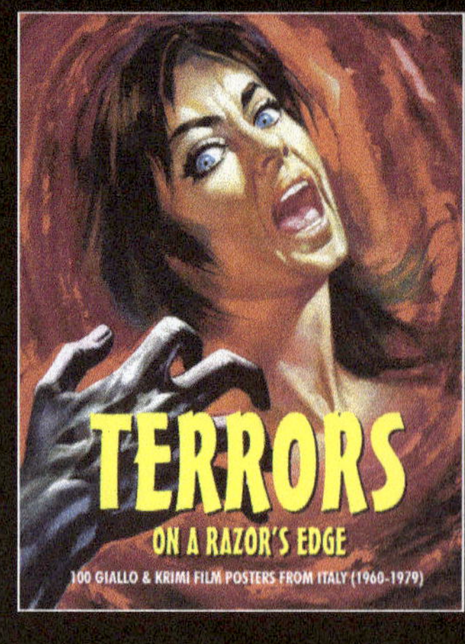
TERRORS
ON A RAZOR'S EDGE
100 GIALLO & KRIMI FILM POSTERS FROM ITALY (1960-1979)

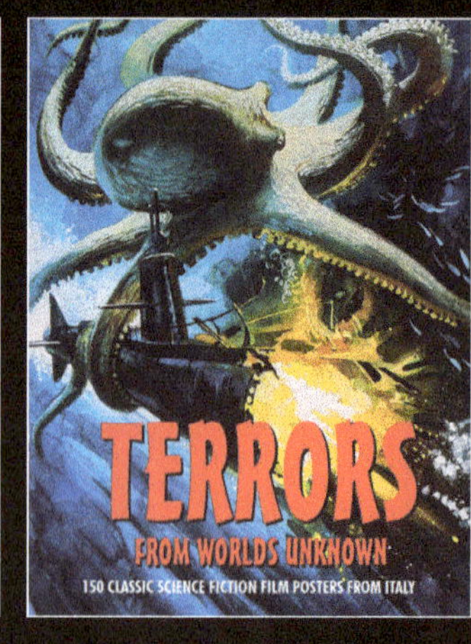
TERRORS
FROM WORLDS UNKNOWN
150 CLASSIC SCIENCE FICTION FILM POSTERS FROM ITALY

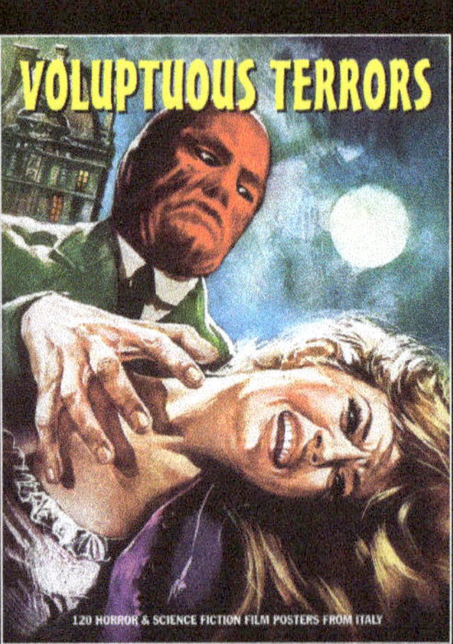
VOLUPTUOUS TERRORS
120 HORROR & SCIENCE FICTION FILM POSTERS FROM ITALY

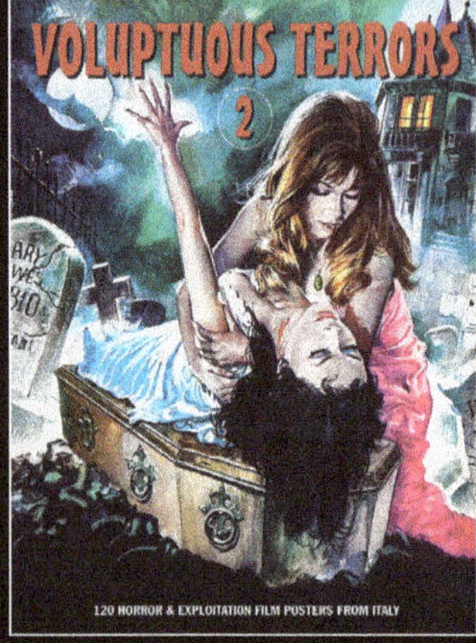
VOLUPTUOUS TERRORS
2
120 HORROR & EXPLOITATION FILM POSTERS FROM ITALY

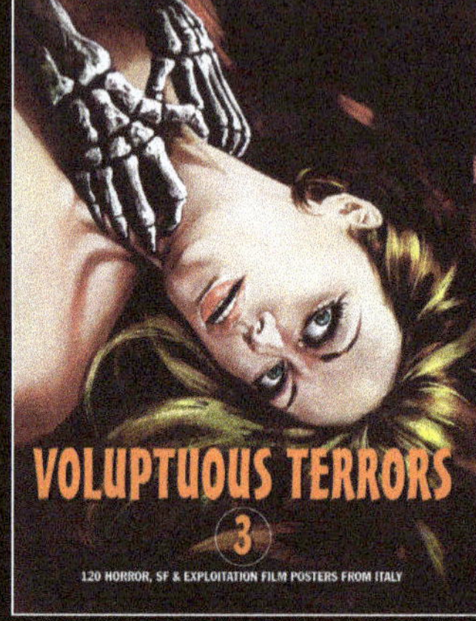
VOLUPTUOUS TERRORS
3
120 HORROR, SF & EXPLOITATION FILM POSTERS FROM ITALY

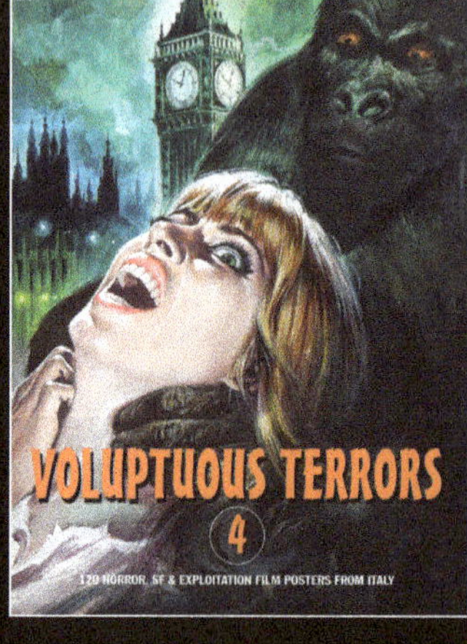
VOLUPTUOUS TERRORS
4
120 HORROR, SF & EXPLOITATION FILM POSTERS FROM ITALY

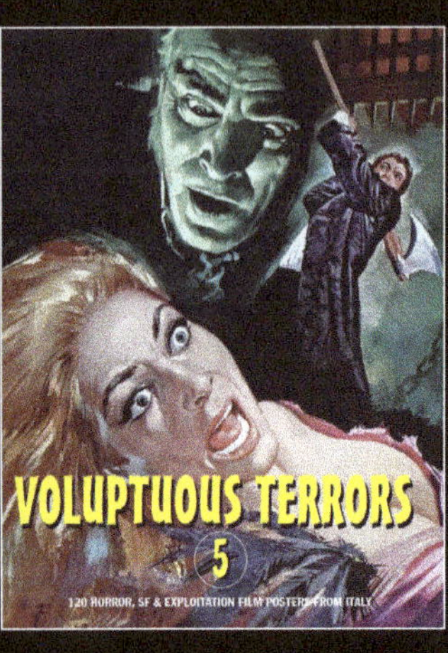
VOLUPTUOUS TERRORS
5
120 HORROR, SF & EXPLOITATION FILM POSTERS FROM ITALY

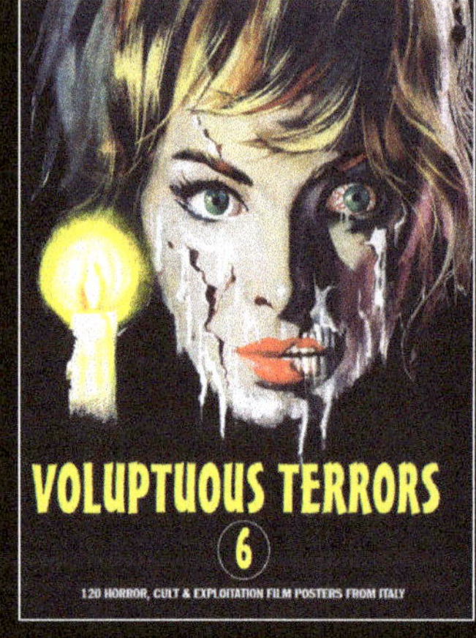
VOLUPTUOUS TERRORS
6
120 HORROR, CULT & EXPLOITATION FILM POSTERS FROM ITALY

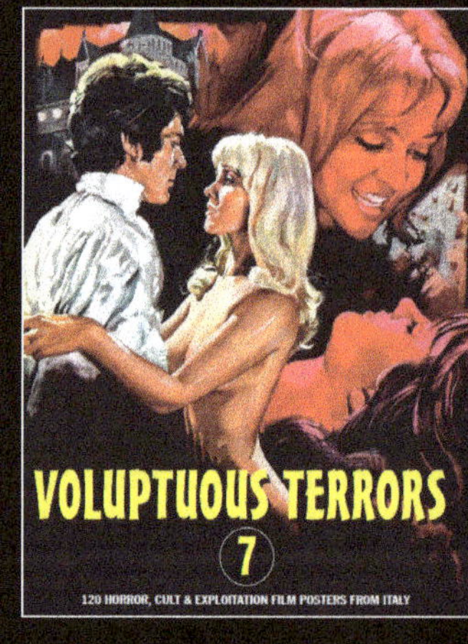
VOLUPTUOUS TERRORS
7
120 HORROR, CULT & EXPLOITATION FILM POSTERS FROM ITALY

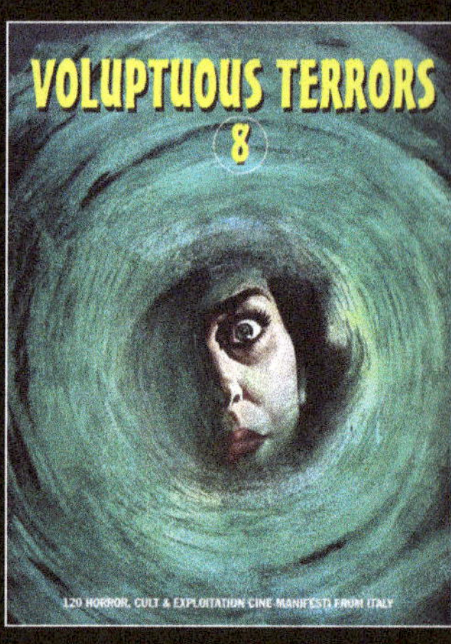
VOLUPTUOUS TERRORS
8
120 HORROR, CULT & EXPLOITATION CINE MANIFESTI FROM ITALY

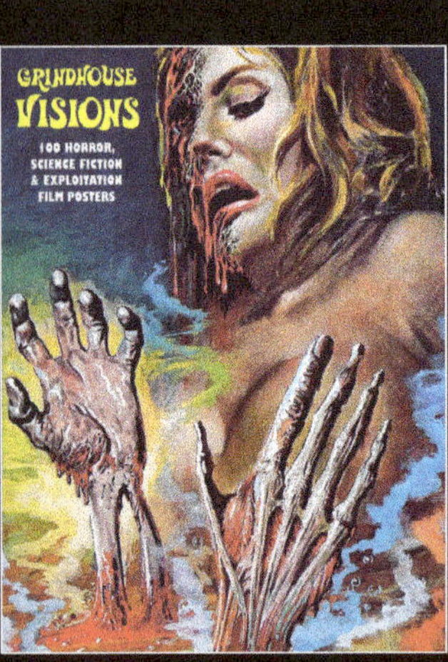
GRINDHOUSE
VISIONS
100 HORROR,
SCIENCE FICTION
& EXPLOITATION
FILM POSTERS

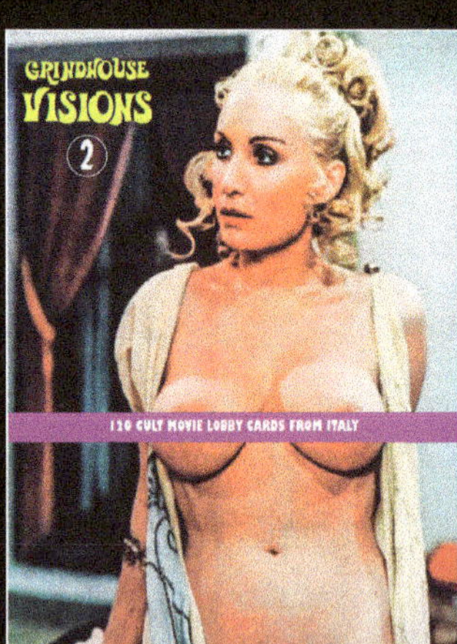
GRINDHOUSE
VISIONS
2
120 CULT MOVIE LOBBY CARDS FROM ITALY

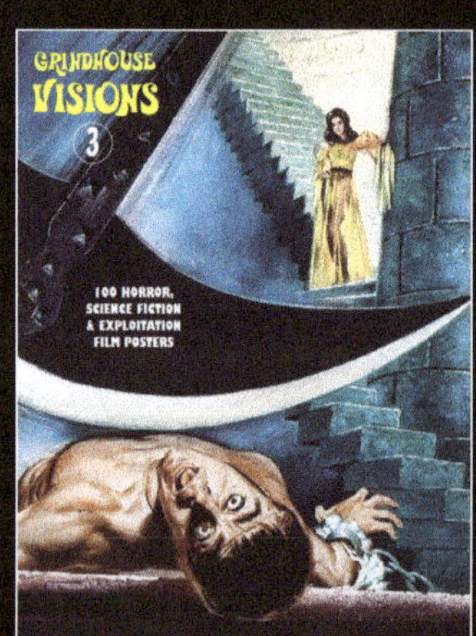
GRINDHOUSE
VISIONS
3
100 HORROR,
SCIENCE FICTION
& EXPLOITATION
FILM POSTERS

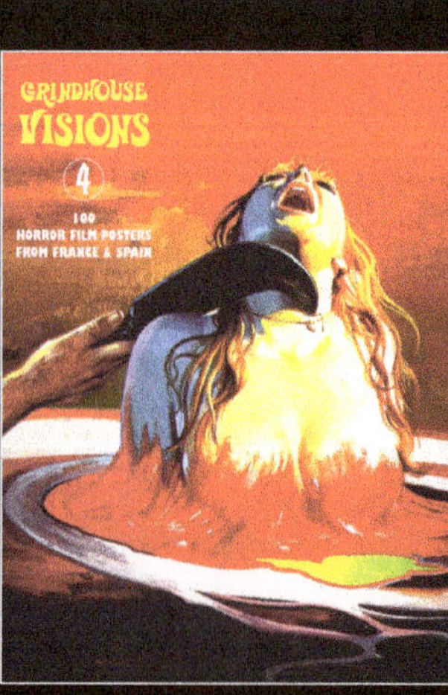
GRINDHOUSE
VISIONS
4
100
HORROR FILM POSTERS
FROM FRANCE & SPAIN